# Birds of the tropics

# Birds of the tropics

Text and photographs by
M. D. England O.B.E.

**Hamlyn**
London · New York · Sydney · Toronto

# Contents

Introduction 5
The Ostrich 13
The Larger Water Birds 18
Birds of Prey 31
Cranes, Gallinules and Bustards 41
Waders, Gulls and Terns 48
Parrots 51
Swifts and Hummingbirds 58
From Kingfishers to Barbets 62
Perching Birds 72
Photographing Birds 83
Books to Read 91
Index 93

*Previous pages* As it sits watching for a movement in the water below, this gorgeous little Malachite Kingfisher bends the leaf on which it is perching little more than would a dragonfly.

The author's photographs are reproduced through the agency of Ardea Photographics, London.

All the photographs which illustrate this book were taken by the author in the birds' native habitat, with the exception of those on pages 32 (bottom), 49, 53, 57, 70, 71 and 88, for permission to photograph which in captivity he is grateful to Mr Len Hill of 'Birdland', Bourton-on-the-Water, and Mr Brian Ward of 'Winged World', Heysham. The photograph on page 84–5 was taken in the author's garden

Published by
THE HAMLYN PUBLISHING GROUP LIMITED
London · New York · Sydney · Toronto
Astronaut House, Feltham, Middlesex, England.
Copyright © The Hamlyn Publishing Group Limited 1974

ISBN 0 600 38685 6

Printed in Czechoslovakia
51674

# Introduction

It is usual to include in the tropics all that part of the world which lies between the Tropic of Cancer in the north and the Tropic of Capricorn in the south, a band 3,000 miles wide and extending for 1,500 miles on either side of the Equator. So far as the distribution of birds is concerned this is a quite unscientific region, but it is a convenient one for a book of this type. As long ago as 1858 the now most generally accepted division of the world into 'faunal regions' was proposed by P.L. Sclater; the map on this page shows those parts of his regions which lie within the tropical zone.

Two of his regions, the Palaearctic, which comprises Europe, North Africa and northern Asia, and the Nearctic, North America above the tropics, do not come into the tropics at all, although parts of all the others do.

Those birds which reside in the tropics do not need to migrate to other parts of the world to escape intolerable weather conditions and so they tend to move, if they move at all, in search of food and the distances involved are usually comparatively slight. On the other hand, since both animal and vegetable food is to be found in

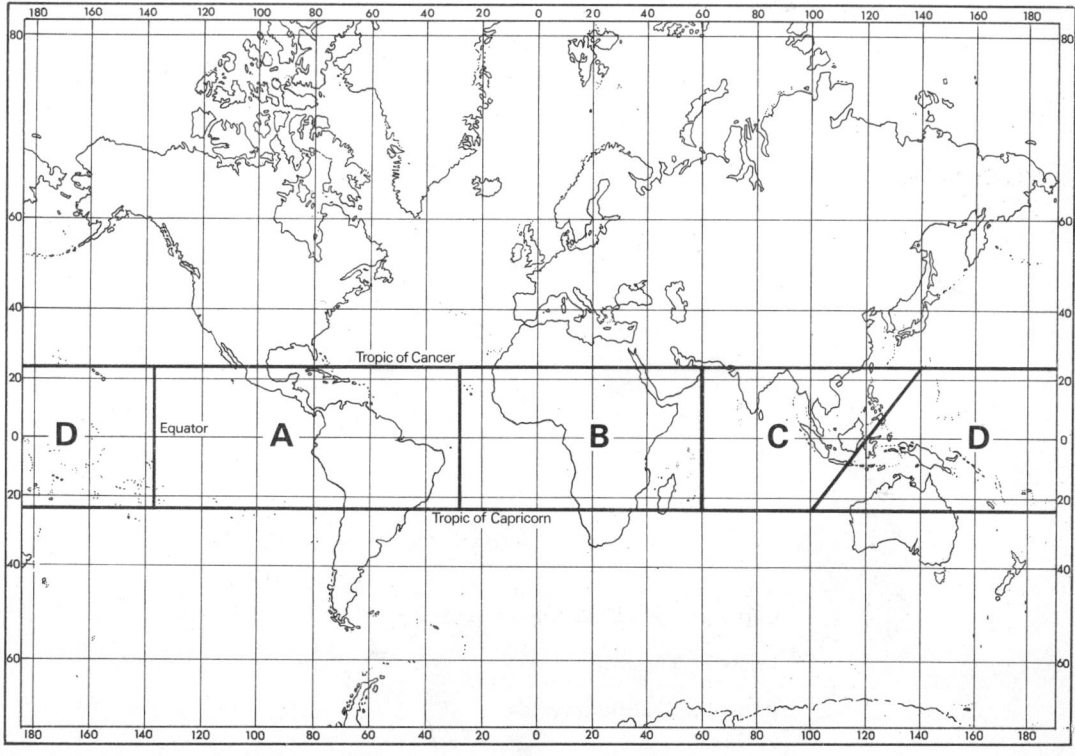

Map of the world, showing the tropics and the divisions used in the list on pp 93–96.
(A = Neotropical;
B = Ethiopian;
C = Oriental;
D = Australasian).

*Far left* **White Pelicans** preening in the tropical sunshine after bathing. The pelican's somewhat grotesque appearance and the well-known couplet about its bill have led to its being thought of as an ugly, clumsy bird, but once airborne there are few large birds with a greater mastery of the air and a soaring flock of pelicans looks superb. In direct flight they usually adopt a line-ahead or V-formation.

*Left* There is a confusing number of species of white egrets over much of the world and matters are made no easier for the inexpert birdwatcher by the fact that in some places four or five species may be seen together. In the tropics the **Little Egret** extends from Africa and Madagascar through India and Ceylon eastwards, with some curious gaps, to Borneo and Australia.
   Egrets have been terribly persecuted for the beautiful feathery plumes which they grow in the breeding season. Miscalled 'osprey plumes' by the millinery trade – they have no connection with Ospreys – these aigrettes were formerly greatly in demand to satisfy the demands of fashion, and egrets were slaughtered by the thousand. This practice has been stopped by the more enlightened countries, but unfortunately even in these countries, thoughtless and selfish women still create a black-market demand which is satisfied chiefly by the countries of northern South America, where the slaughter still goes on.

*Below* **Darters** – also called Anhingas, Water Turkeys or Snake Birds – are found in tropical Africa, Asia and south-east to the Philippines, New Guinea and Australia, in addition to many parts of the New World. Unlike their close relatives the cormorants they catch their food – mainly fish – by spearing rather than grabbing it, rising to the surface to shake it off their bill, catch and swallow it.

greater abundance in the tropics than elsewhere, the concentration of birds in this zone is very high indeed at certain times of the year, because the residents are joined by immense numbers of visitors which have flown south to avoid bad winter weather and lack of food in those countries where they have spent the summer. A few have moved north to the tropics.

Birds are divided scientifically into 'orders', which are subdivided into 'families', and such a large number of families, let alone species, is to be found in the tropics at one or other time of the year that it would be impossible in a book of ninety-six pages even to mention them all, quite apart from describing or illustrating them. The problem of selection is therefore a very difficult one for the author of such a book. Birds may be arbitrarily chosen because they are especially attractive or striking in plumage, shape or habit; because they are rare or are not usually mentioned, except in books for the specialist; or even because they are already familiar as common exhibits in zoos. The present author is all too well aware of the stools between which he may fall and that his selection is open to criticism on many grounds, not the least of which is the omission of species – indeed, of families – which it might reasonably have been expected would be included. The choice of illustration was necessarily limited to those species of which he had taken adequate photographs, and so far as possible those described in the text are birds with which he is familiar. More important, preference has been given to those birds (or their close relatives) which are likely to be seen by any interested person who has the good fortune to visit the appropriate part of the world. More and more people are becoming aware of wildlife, and world travel – either for pleasure or business – is commonplace. One does not need to be an ornithologist to enjoy the birds around one's home, but this enjoyment is greatly enhanced if one has some idea what they are and a little knowledge of their often very interesting way of life. This is even more the case when away from home, especially when visiting somewhere as exciting as a tropical country. However, it must be said at once that this is NOT a 'Field Guide to the Birds of the Tropics'; far from it. It should be regarded as no more than an appetizer. Included are just a few of the birds which it will hardly be possible to miss, or which are worth looking for, in some of the easily-accessible parts of the tropics; no elaborate ornithological safari will be needed for most of them, although it has to be admitted that a few, such as the Cock-of-the-rock, which no ordinary traveller is likely to see, have been included for interest or beauty's sake or because their omission would have been unforgiveable indeed, whatever the approach to the subject.

Many kinds of habitat are found in the tropics and each has its characteristic birds, which have become adapted to exploit to the full the capacity of a particular place to provide food and breeding sites without too intense competition with other species. Scorching desert or steamy jungle immediately come to mind in association with tropical countries, but this is only a small part of the truth. Savanna and more or less open forest or woodland account for huge areas; marshes and swamps occupy large tracts and pure grassland covers smaller areas. As habitats, lakes and rivers and their environs are very important, mangrove swamps for example having a huge bird population. The oceans, too, provide a feeding ground for immense numbers of sea birds which must, however, return to land to breed.

The capacity of a type of habitat to support a particular species of bird depends upon its ability to supply one or other, or both, of two requirements: food and suitable nesting-places. It might be added that the habitat must also have a climate which is not intolerable because of extremes, but in most cases this is synonymous with its ability to provide food. The question of successful competition with other species is an important one but is too profound for a book of this type.

Some species of bird are sedentary, or comparatively so. It has already been noted, for instance, that those birds which breed in the tropics do not, generally speaking, need to move away after the breeding season; others breed in one habitat and spend the rest of the year in another.

So far as the range of foodstuffs taken by birds is concerned, it has been said with truth that 'birds have exploited all that grows and moves upon the surface of the earth and in the upper layer of all its waters', and it could hardly have been better expressed. Some birds are virtually omnivorous, for example crows and some species of gulls, while others are very specialized, like the Everglade Kite which appears to eat only one particular kind of snail. There are species, such as some finches, which eat insects in the summer and seeds in the winter; and others eat insects when young and seeds when adult. In order to deal with this wide range of food, birds have developed an astonishing variety of bills. Small insect-eating birds usually have small, slender bills, though some flycatchers have flattened bills to enable them more easily to seize a flying insect. Most hummingbirds have developed long, slim, curved bills which enable them to obtain insects and nectar from deep within flowers.

The strong, hooked bills of birds of prey are familiar to all as instruments for seizing, killing and tearing up the flesh of their prey. The toucans of the New World and the hornbills of the Old have bills which are large (sometimes disproportionately so), often brightly coloured, and look heavy and unwieldy, although they are light for their size and useful for reaching out and grasping fruit growing on slender branches. It would seem that a long, slim bill would have achieved this equally well, and the reason for these rather grotesquely shaped ones, which give the birds such an ungainly appearance, is not known.

Many birds regurgitate undigested food in the form of 'pellets', egg-shaped masses of fur and bones which in some cases seem uncomfortably large for the birds to bring up. In some species they are in fact larger than the items of food which the birds habitually eat. That the ejection of a pellet is not altogether a comfortable proceeding may be seen from the fact that the bird often looks quite sickly for some time before it happens. Many people familiar with birds in captivity will remember the great relief which they felt on the first occasion that they witnessed the emission of a pellet, because they had feared the bird to be really ill. It used to be thought that pellets were only produced by birds of prey and always consisted of bones (often complete skulls), fur and feathers. It is now known that a wide variety of birds do this habitually, their pellets containing fish scales, insect legs and wing-cases, seeds, fruit skins and almost anything which the bird has swallowed but is unable to digest completely. It is interesting that the digestive powers of some young birds are greater than those of their parents, since pellet-production may not start when they are nestlings and it is most unlikely that some of the bulkier waste matter is able to pass the complete length of the alimentary canal.

If it be true that birds have explored the possibilities of everything that could conceivably be described as 'food', it is equally true that they have taken advantage of all possible places in which to rear their families, and nowhere is there so diverse a range of sites than in the tropics. Eggs may be laid almost anywhere from the bare ground to a chamber within a most elaborately constructed nest. Many nests are briefly described in the text, but especially interesting examples are the floating or semi-floating nests of grebes, the little mud cups of flamingos (tiny in relation to the bird), and the wonderfully-woven hanging nests of some weavers (often entered from the bottom as a protection against marauding snakes). The device by which some swifts use a salivary secretion to glue their eggs to the leaves of palm trees is also of great interest.

It has been estimated that there are about 100,000 million birds in the world, but it will be appreciated that, although based on what is known about bird population, this figure can be little more than an inspired guess. There are some 8,600 species but there seem to be no reliable figures for the number of species which breed in the tropics, while the task of compiling an accurate list of those which *occur* in the tropics is an almost impossible one, bearing in mind the visitors from other areas and the inaccessibility of much of the terrain. However, as mentioned above, it can be said with some certainty that the density of the bird population in the tropical region is very high compared with other zoographical regions, and that the greatest number of species within the tropics is to be found in Central and South America.

Although the buildings of civilized man have provided nesting-sites for some species and agriculture has provided a certain amount of food for others, and although it may reasonably be argued that telephone wires and electricity pylons have benefited and assisted the spread of some species by providing singing-posts and perches from which to watch for prey in country which previously lacked them, on balance man is the worst enemy that birds have. He destroys them in immense numbers for food, or for their feathers, or because he believes, rightly or wrongly, that they are harmful to him; he traps many as pets and he takes their eggs and even their nests for

*Far left* **Saddlebill Stork**, photographed at Buffalo Springs, Northern Territory, Kenya. Although many storks are gregarious, Saddlebills tend to live solitary lives and even when nesting they do not gather into large colonies as many storks do. Most of them nest on the ground, often among reedbeds. The bird is easily recognised by its large size — it stands more than four feet high — its black and white plumage, and its extraordinary black, red and yellow bill with the coloured 'saddle' near its base.

The **Painted Stork** of Asia (*above*) and **Yellow-billed** of Africa (*left*) are closely related and rather similar in appearance. Although looking mainly white from a distance, the African bird especially may be seen to have a beautiful pink flush if one can approach close enough.

In the photograph the Painted Storks are busily feeding in an Indian swamp, with a large Black-necked Stork behind and egrets in the foreground, while the solitary Yellow-billed (sometimes miscalled the Wood Ibis) is resting beside an African lake.

food; but man's greatest impact on bird-life has been, and is increasingly, the direct one of the destruction of their natural habitat. The cutting down of vast areas of forest, cultivation of the land on a huge scale, the drainage of swamps and the spread of towns all mean the reduction – sometimes the extinction – of very many species and it is estimated that still, despite the welcome growth of human interest in protection and conservation, an average of one species of bird is lost to the world each year. By his indiscriminate use of untried pesticides, the consequences of which he did not even pause to consider, man has so contaminated the environment that few, if any birds are immune to their devastating effects. Even lakes, rivers and the oceans are now polluted to a degree which must horrify all but the most callous. The destruction of untold numbers of sea birds by oil slicks is dreadful and dramatic, but the more subtle and largely still not fully understood results of the broadcasting of toxic chemicals by hand, machine, and, worst of all, from the air decimates wildlife on a scale which is inestimable.

However, on the credit side is the great upsurge, in many civilized parts of the world, of an interest in nature and in living creatures, with the result that depredation is deplored and great efforts made to stem the tide of destruction. Man has traditionally thought of conservation as a process by which he presumed to 'protect' certain species (usually those in which he had an especial interest, for purposes of food or sport) by the ruthless elimination of those creatures which he considered in his ignorance to be their enemies, and which he classed as 'vermin'. In particular, every man's hand has been against birds of prey, which have been relentlessly harried almost everywhere by game-keepers, farmers and so-called 'sportsmen' who exhibit a most extraordinary unwillingness to accept the fact that predators are not only a natural part of the ecological balance but that even their own aim of the preservation of the particular species in which they take an interest for their own purposes is best served by the presence of an appropriate population of predators. Not least of the reasons for this is the fact that predators tend to prey more upon the sick or weaker members of a species and thus serve the very useful purpose of helping to ensure that the surviving population is a strong and healthy one. It has even been demonstrated that predators can in certain instances actually increase the numbers of the particular species on which they prey.

Modern thought on conservation has swung away from destruction of natural enemies towards the concept that birds and other animals will thrive if they are left alone in a suitable habitat, which must include food, water (in most cases), suitable cover and nesting-sites, conditions which satisfy important aspects of behaviour such as singing-posts and lek arenas, and sufficient space. The emphasis has thus been focused on the preservation of the habitat, and the almost world-wide creation of reserves and national parks is most encouraging. Public opinion and societies formed for the protection of birds are now in many countries sufficiently powerful to influence governments, however tardily, but whether public opinion can, in the long term, override the interests of 'big business' (for example the production of oil, pesticides, fertilizers and plastics) has yet to be seen. It seems likely that only the awakening of man to the fact that he is destroying himself at the same time as other creatures will stem the tide of his misuse of his environment.

# The Ostrich

The Ostrich, which was once widespread over Africa, is the largest species of living bird, not only in the tropics but in the entire world. Everyone must be familiar with its appearance, its long neck surmounted by a curiously small head and its long, bare and tremendously powerful legs. Everyone must know, too, of its 'plumes', for which it has been farmed in South Africa for many years, the plumes being cut for sale about every eight months on average. Males have a black body with white tail and wings; females are grey-brown and have a rather dingy appearance. The bare skin on the necks and legs of the males is pink or grey according to the area from which they come. The Ostrich is distinguished from all the other families of birds by having only two toes. It cannot fly.

A full-grown male stands nearly eight feet tall and can run at forty miles per hour or more. The female is slightly smaller but is still a most impressive bird. Although sometimes found in pairs they are usually polygamous, each male having about three females, all of which lay their eggs in the same nest, which is merely an area where the grass has been trampled down or a hollow scraped out of the ground.

Each female lays six to eight eggs, so that twenty eggs or even more are found in one nest. The male takes a large share of the duties of incubation, brooding all night, but he is relieved for periods during the day by the hens. The eggs take a little less than six weeks to hatch and the young chicks, which are greyish-brown with black stripes on their head and neck, are very mobile immediately after hatching and at a month old have been known to run at thirty-five miles an hour.

Hatching success is poor because so many predators manage to break and eat the eggs, and it is largely because of the agility of the newly hatched chick that Ostriches have survived. Although they have natural enemies, especially when young, man is the worst enemy of all. Once widespread in Africa, most wild Ostriches that are alive today are either in National Parks or in a few very remote and arid districts.

The natural habitat of the Ostrich varies from desert wastes to bushy savanna. Although it used to be said that it can live in completely barren desert, this is not true, since it depends for both food and water on vegetation, however sparse. Its food is varied and it eats berries, shrubs, greenery of many kinds, succulents and fallen fruit, as well as lizards and other small animals. When searching for food it roams for considerable distances and its food supply is of course to some extent governed by the weather, as is also its breeding season, which usually coincides with or immediately follows the rainy season. The Ostrich is often to be seen consorting with parties of mammals such as warthogs, gazelles and zebras.

The Ostrich is replaced in South America by the Rhea, and in Australia by the Cassowary and Emu. All are closely related and all are flightless; but unlike the Ostrich, the Rhea, Cassowary and Emu have three toes. The Rhea has the curious habit when running, and it can run very fast, of lifting one wing so that it looks like a small sail on a ship, but it does not always run away from

*Above left* About a third of the world's population of flamingos are **Lesser Flamingos** which gather in vast hordes on saline lakes in India and Africa. Sometimes over a million birds may be seen together. It has rightly been said that one of the most wonderful — not to say staggering — ornithological experiences is to see the flamingos on Lake Nakuru in the Rift Valley, Kenya. The shores of this lake are lined, further than the eye can see, with a broad mass of birds (both Lesser and Greater Flamingos, though far more of the former) which literally reach over the million mark at some times of the year.

In this photograph may be seen a very small section of the Lesser Flamingos engaged in their extraordinary 'parade', in which they march, now this way now that, as though at words of command, each bird jostling the one ahead as if urgently needing to get closer and ever closer, though never losing the appearance of a controlled and orderly parade. Although not directly concerned with individual courtship, and on Lake Nakuru performed in a place where they do not breed, this seems to effect a stimulus to the flock immediately before the rather unpredictable and sporadic breeding takes place.

*Left* In dull light a sombrely-clad, almost black, bird, sunshine brings out the beautiful colours in the plumage of the **Glossy Ibis**. In part of its range it overlaps a rather similar bird, the Hadada Ibis, so-called because of its repeated laughing call 'ha-da-da' as it flies over. However, the latter may be distinguished by the red on the upper side of the base of its bill and a white streak below its cheeks. The Glossy Ibis has an extraordinarily patchy and widespread distribution over the world and a map of its tropical range would include some of the West Indian Islands, a small patch in East Africa, two or three in Asia — including small colonies in India — south-east to a restricted area at the northern tip of Australia. Rather curiously, it is widespread in Madagascar.

*Above* The **Sacred Ibis** was held sacred by the ancient Egyptians who named it Thoth, the scribe of the gods. Despite frequent bathing and preening, the black plumes on its lower back nearly always look somewhat unkempt. The preening is accompanied by much wing-flapping and holding the wings aloft, when the narrow black border of the white wings is seen at its best. Although long since driven away from Egypt, in some places in Africa this bird has become very fearless of man, sitting about on roof-tops and even feeding from scraps dropped by diners at open-air restaurants.

danger and will crouch down and stay still if the cover is sufficient.

The Cassowary, although still a large bird, is smaller than its relations and differs from them in living in jungle rather than in more open country. It has the reputation of being dangerous if surprised or cornered and there have been a number of instances of people being killed by them.

The Emu is next in size to the Ostrich and, despite the fact that in parts of Australia it is considered to be a serious pest to agriculture, it has survived remarkably well. In 1932 the Commonwealth Government was prevailed upon to wage war on the farmer's enemy, which they did quite literally by sending a machine-gun unit in an attempt at destruction on a large scale. The campaign was a complete and ridiculous failure and was made to appear all the more so by the fact that newspapers had reporters in the 'front line' to send daily despatches about the progress of the war. By the time that the Royal Australian Artillery made contact with the reported 20,000 birds which had invaded the farmland, the 'enemy', instead of ranging themselves on a mass front as a target, had split into innumerable small parties over a wide area which made the use of machine-guns quite uneconomic. After about a month of almost complete failure the troops were withdrawn and appeals to the Government to send them again were ignored. The erection of fences across the Emus' seasonal migration routes, along which they move in search of food in the wheat-growing country, proved much more successful and, although controlled, the bird is now in no immediate danger of extermination.

**Greater Flamingos** are gregarious by nature and usually feed in parties and breed in large colonies. This solitary bird was photographed in a quiet backwater of an African lake and seen close to like this it is difficult to escape the feeling that, however lovely a picture a flock makes at a distance, the head and bill are grotesque rather than beautiful.

# The Larger Water Birds

All birds are of course dependent on water for life. Some, like the Ostrich in the last chapter, obtain a large proportion of the fluid which they need from the plants on which they feed, and spend much of their lives many miles from lakes or rivers. Others – and there are a great many of these – spend most of their lives near water because they are dependent on it to supply not only drink but food; some are never away from water except when flying from one stretch to another.

Grebes are a good example of the last type. They feed on fish and other small aquatic creatures and have become so specialized that they cannot perch at all and, except for a few of the smallest species which are rather more agile, can scarcely support themselves on their feet on land; the best they can do is an awkward, rather staggering shuffle, and this only when climbing out of the water on to their nest. This also is very specialized, being constructed in the water from a mass of sodden, floating or semi-floating vegetation, with which the eggs are often covered when the sitting bird leaves the nest. Both sexes share in incubation and tending the young, and both take part in the courtship display which in some species is a very elaborate ritual, including upright dances in the water, weed-holding, head-shaking and rushes across the water. Some are solitary nesters, others form colonies – sometimes of very considerable size – and may mix with terns and gulls for breeding purposes. This may be of benefit to the grebes since the air-borne gulls are able to act as 'watch-dogs' and give early warning of approaching danger which might not be seen from the surface of the water. Although most – though not all – species of grebe are able to fly, they rarely do so when alarmed, preferring to dive. All species can remain under water for a considerable time and some, even when they do need to surface, remain virtually invisible until they are assured that danger is past by showing only enough of their head for the bill and eyes to be above water.

Grebes are found almost all over the world and some species are very widespread in their distribution, occurring not only in the tropics but far north and south of this area. A few, on the other hand, are restricted to high mountain lakes in South America. Visitors to the tropical parts of the Old World who go near inland water can hardly avoid seeing the Little Grebe which, apart from being the commonest grebe all over Europe except the far north, occurs right across tropical Africa, India, throughout Burma, down to New Guinea and other islands, and in Australia is represented by an almost indistinguishable cousin. At some times of the year it is so numerous along the shores of the famous Lake Nakuru in Kenya that it is almost impossible to take a photograph of another species on the shore without the background being spoiled by black spots, which are out-of-focus Little Grebes.

The Black-necked and Great Crested Grebes are also widespread in Europe but at the same time breed in the tropics, the former in tropical East Africa and the latter right across tropical Africa, to reappear in Queensland, where the northern end of its range in eastern Australia just takes it into the tropics. In the New World the most widespread grebe is the Red-billed which occurs in North, Central and South America.

All grebes lay white or slightly green-tinted eggs, but these more often than not appear to be a dirty brown colour because they soon become stained by the damp rotting vegetation of which the nest is made. Incubation is by both sexes, the returning bird often bringing a token offering of weed which is added to the nest, and both male and female feed and care for the striped, downy young, which, when small, they frequently carry on their backs. If the parent is forced to dive, the chicks which it is carrying often pop-up to the surface like corks, although they may be carried under water for a considerable distance, held by the parent's wings.

Grebes have the curious habit, the reason for which is not known, although it presumably has to do with digestion, of swallowing quite a large number of their own feathers and even of offering them to their young.

If most people are familiar with the appearance of an Ostrich, they are probably just as much so with a pelican, but what a vast difference there is between the two. The Ostrich is tall, long-legged, small-billed and flightless; the pelican is squat, very short-legged, has a large bill made to look larger still by the distensible pouch beneath it, and is a superb flier.

Pelicans spend most of their life near water and are among the world's largest birds. There are half a dozen or so species, widely distributed in the tropics and in some of the more temperate parts of the world. Most pelicans are mainly white with wings which are dark-tipped, but one of the two American species is the Brown Pelican, which differs from its relatives in catching the fish on which it feeds by diving from the air into the sea. Other members of the family catch their food by quietly swimming around, usually in parties, and periodically dipping their bills in the water all together, as though at a given signal, until suddenly the whole 'raft' of birds turns inwards and starts to feed, apparently having surrounded a shoal of fish.

Although it looks an effort for pelicans to rise from either land or water, once they are airborne they fly very strongly, with the head retracted – not extended like cranes and storks. They may sometimes be seen soaring at a great height, wheeling slowly round and round getting even higher, until they are above the evening sun and are lit up underneath by a rosy glow.

Pelicans breed in colonies, sometimes on the ground and sometimes in trees; nests on the ground are usually comparatively simple affairs made of reeds or other vegetation, sticks or even mud. Tree nests are large and are made of sticks. The eggs are a chalky-looking pale blue or white and incubation takes about a month. On hatching, young pelicans look remarkably reptilian, being naked and black and having short very un-pelican-like bills. They soon acquire a downy covering and their bills do not take long to grow; they feed by thrusting their heads into the parent's open bill. The pouch is used for catching and straining fish, not storing them, and there is some disagreement as to whether young pelicans feed from the pouch or from their parent's gullet. It seems probable that, like for example, young cormorants, they push their bill well down the parent's throat, but this does not preclude them finding some of the regurgitated food in the pouch as well.

Those species of pelican most likely to be seen in the tropics are the Brown around Central America (including the Galapagos Islands); the White in Africa, possibly near the north-west coast of India, and out of the breeding season as far south-east as the Philippines; and the Pink-backed in Africa (this and the White are the species to be seen in some of the African National Parks). In Australia and the islands to the north is the Australian Pelican, which has much more black in its plumage than the other 'white' pelicans.

If pelicans appear reptilian when they are young, cormorants do so all their lives. They are dark in colour and their feathers in some lights look remarkably like scales. They have long necks, and have the habit of sitting drying their half-extended wings in a way which, even if not exactly reptilian, looks for all the world as though it were the artist's impression of some prehistoric creature in our school biology books.

Cormorants are aquatic birds which live on coastal waters almost all over the world and on many lakes and rivers far inland. Most of them are black with a metallic sheen of blue or green and some have white on their throat or breast. Although they live near water and are wonderful swimmers they spend a great deal of their time out of the water, entering it chiefly to catch fish

*Above* The beautiful **White-faced Tree Duck** is found in tropical South America, Africa and Madagascar. It is usually a rather shy and unapproachable bird which is unwilling to allow a close enough approach for photography; this is a lucky shot taken from a car beside Lake Edward in Uganda, after much careful and clever manoeuvring by the driver.

*Right* The **Black-shouldered Kite** is a beautiful little hawk found in many parts of the world, and may be seen in all four of our divisions of the tropics. A very few even reach Europe to breed in southern Portugal. Although mainly a bird of open country, in some parts of Australia it may be seen well inside towns watching from roof-tops and overhead wires for mice and large insects even in the heat of the day, despite the fact that its eyes are adapted for hunting in poor light.

which make up the main part of their food. Their bills are hooked for catching and holding their prey, which they chase underwater, sometimes reaching a considerable depth; they nearly always rise to the surface before swallowing what they have caught. Although their wings are comparatively small and they appear to have difficulty in rising, they fly quite strongly. Over water they fly quite low but when flying over land they usually rise much higher. Cormorants nest in colonies, either on rocks, cliffs or in trees. Nests which are near the sea are mostly made of seaweed, and in the absence of this, sticks or all kinds of vegetation may be used. They lay two to four or more pale greenish-blue eggs and both parents share incubation and feeding of the young.

There are about thirty species of cormorant. The large Common Cormorant ranges from Canada in the north to New Zealand in the south (though it is absent from South America), occurring in the tropics in Africa, India and northern Australia. There are four species which are much smaller than the rest of the family and have relatively longer tails: they are called Pygmy, Little, Long-tailed and Little Pied Cormorants. One species, found in the Galapagos Islands, is flightless.

Darters, or Snake Birds, are if anything even more reptile-like than cormorants, since they frequently swim with only the head and neck above water, making snaky, writhing, to-and-fro movements of the neck. Like cormorants they live on fish which they pursue under water, but they differ in having a sharp pointed bill, not a hooked one, with which they frequently spear their prey rather than grabbing it. Once above water with a fish they toss it in the air, to catch and swallow it head first.

Darters are not sea birds but live on rivers and lakes, usually those with wooded banks where they sit on dead trees or half submerged logs or rocks, holding their wings out to dry. Another difference from cormorants is that their plumage, instead of appearing to be scaly, tends to look bedraggled and unkempt. The Darter is more nearly restricted to the tropics than the cormorant, and in mid-America it is called the Anhinga and sometimes the Water Turkey. It breeds in colonies, nesting in trees near or growing out of the water.

Frigate birds, sometimes called man-of-war birds, are large, mainly black sea birds with enormous wings and forked tails. They obtain most of their food by chasing other birds and compelling them to disgorge; then most skilfully catching the food in mid-air. They are able to fish for themselves although they are not very willing to do so because their plumage readily becomes waterlogged, and they not infrequently take the small young of other birds, such as terns. When they do fish for themselves they usually do so by flying low over the water to catch flying-fish or when necessary plunging just below the surface.

There are five species of frigate bird, with a number of sub-species, and all are found in tropical or sub-tropical waters, seldom far from the islands on which they breed. Although they are occasionally found wandering far from home, the sight of two or three frigate birds has always been regarded by mariners as an indication that land cannot be far away.

The plumage is mainly black and there is a striking difference between the sexes, especially during the breeding season when males develop a remarkable crimson inflatable sac under the bill. Frigate birds are colonial nesters, building either on the ground or in trees and bushes. At the start of the breeding season the males take up a nest site and perform a frenzied display, with sac inflated and wings spread, in order to attract a mate from the females flying overhead. Both sexes build the nest, incubate the single white egg, and feed the chick, which is dependent upon its parents for a long time. In some species this period may last up to six months.

Herons and egrets are medium- to large-sized birds with long legs and necks and slim bodies; most of them have long, straight, pointed bills, and they fly with their legs extended behind them but the neck retracted. Some species are entirely white while others have mixtures of rather sober colours. Many of them grow long plumes on the head, neck and back, especially in the breeding season. Most species live near water and many wade for their food; some, however, wait motionless by the water's edge until prey comes close, when they seize it by a sudden swift downwards plunge of the bill. Others – for example the large Grey Heron on the one hand and the small Green Heron on the other – will often dive for their food from a perch above the water. In the former case the perch is sometimes in a tree at a considerable height, but the dive is a somewhat clumsy affair and it is surprising that the prey is not given sufficient warning to enable it to escape.

The Cattle Egret, sometimes called the Buff-backed Heron, is a white bird which acquires buff plumes in the breeding season. It gets its name from its habit of associating with mammals in order to catch the insects and other creatures which they disturb as they move about while grazing. They may be seen near both domestic and wild mammals and in the tropics it is by no means uncommon to see them perched on the backs of elephants and rhinos, although when actually feeding they usually walk around the mammals' feet.

The Little and Yellow-billed Egrets are also white birds, the latter being almost confined to tropical countries while the former spreads from the tropics northward to southern Europe and southward as far as South Africa and eastern Australia. The Yellow-billed is sometimes called the Intermediate or Middle Egret because of the confusion caused by the fact that several other species have yellow bills and because it is intermediate in size between the Little and Great Egrets, both of which are also found in tropical countries.

The Black Heron of tropical Africa has a most interesting method of feeding. It stands in shallow water with its wings raised and brought forward over the head to form an 'umbrella', which shades a patch of water over which the bill is poised ready to dart at a fish which swims by. It is not certain whether the object of the shade is to lure the fish into what it presumes is shelter or to cut out the reflection from the surface of the water and thus make the bird's attack more accurate. Possibly it serves both purposes, though the latter is more likely because a close relation, the Reddish Egret of tropical America, which also raises its wings while fishing, catches its food by making short rapid runs in the water, raising its 'screen' each time it stops, thus giving prey little time to take advantage of the shade, but undoubtedly reducing dazzle. The Black Stork is another bird which does this.

The Night Heron, a comparatively small member of the family with a shorter neck and generally rather 'dumpy' appearance, feeds chiefly at night and has developed most beautiful large amber eyes for this purpose. It has several close relations, most of them very similar in appearance.

Most herons and egrets nest colonially, sometimes in large numbers, and the colonies often consist of several different species. The majority of nests – built chiefly of sticks – are in trees or bushes, though some are built in reed-beds or on the ground. Both sexes share in the duties of hatching out and rearing the young, which are fed by regurgitation of partly-digested food. This is dribbled out of the side of the parent's bill which is gripped sideways by the chick.

Herons share with a very few other birds – such as toucans and parrots – a curious characteristic known as the production of 'powder down'. This is a dusty substance which occurs in patches in the plumage (in herons in the breast and on each side of the lower back) and is used by the birds in cleaning themselves. It is of course especially useful to herons after they have been feeding on fish or eels.

Storks are large – sometimes very large – birds with long necks and legs and long, stout bills; some species stand over four feet high. Most species live in the tropics, although two, the White Stork and the Black Stork, breed in Europe. They are strong fliers, mainly flying with neck and legs extended, and some of them perform most wonderful feats of soaring. They live almost entirely on animal food, such as locusts, lizards, frogs and fish, although the Marabou and its relatives are chiefly carrion eaters. These gather at rubbish dumps and, in the company of vultures, around carcasses. Having the neck and head naked, they avoid soiling their feathers.

Storks, with few exceptions, build with sticks large nests which sometimes become immense structures as they are added to year by year. A few nest on the ground, while the Hammerhead – a dull brownish bird from tropical Africa – builds a huge roofed-in nest of sticks and reeds, lined with mud or dung and having a side entrance tunnel. It is built in a tree, often – though not always – near water. This bird also has the unusual habit of perching on the back of a hippopotamus, from which it flops down into the water to catch frogs and other swimming creatures. It gets its name from the tapering backward-pointing crest which, with the broad pointed bill, makes the head the shape of a hammer or, more truly, of a pick or an anvil.

Another 'odd-man-out' is the Shoebill or Whale-headed Stork, also from tropical Africa. This is a tall, dark greyish bird with a large head and an enormous and quite disproportionate bill which is reputedly

**White-backed Vultures** are seen here disputing the pickings from a carcass with a dog, near a main road in India. Vultures serve a very useful purpose as scavengers, clearing up rubbish and putrefying matter which would otherwise remain as the breeding-place of flies and disease.

*Top* An **Augur Buzzard** as it sits watching for prey from road-side telegraph poles is the bird of prey most likely to be noticed by visitors to East Africa. Mainly black and white, it shows its beautiful orange tail as it flies away on the approach of a car.

*Above* The **Long-crested Eagle** (sometimes called Hawk-eagle) is another frequenter of road-side telegraph poles. By the uninitiated it is often mistaken for a cockatoo on account of its crest. Although at rest it looks entirely black, in flight a white patch shows in each wing.

used for 'trowelling-out' fish buried in the muddy bottom of the swamps where it lives. It is one of the few storks which nest on the ground.

Two of the most striking storks – each in its way may fairly be described as beautiful – are the Saddlebill and the so-called Wood Ibis, a very poor and misleading name given to a bird which is a stork and not an ibis and is better called the Yellow-billed Stork. These are two more inhabitants of tropical Africa (the latter having a very similar counterpart in Asia known as the Painted Stork) and their appearance can be much better appreciated from their pictures (pages 10 and 11) than from any description in words.

Ibises are long-billed, long-legged birds with very much the shape and stance of a curlew, although most species are larger. They vary widely in colour, some being mainly white, while others are dark with a lovely metallic sheen. One, the Scarlet Ibis which lives in the northern tropical belt of South America, lives up to its name and is a very lovely bird indeed. Its plumage is bright scarlet all over, and the sight of hundreds of these birds coming in to roost in the swamps, just before dusk, is quite unforgettable. The most widespread of the ibises, the Glossy, is another very lovely member of the family, although it does not always give this impression. At a distance or at first sight in dull light it may appear merely black or a dull, dirty brown, but when seen closely or in sunshine it has a most wonderful gloss of metallic-looking dark green, purple or bronze.

The Sacred Ibis is the bird which was revered by the ancient Egyptians and appears in their mural paintings and sculptures. Today it is no longer found in Egypt but has retreated to tropical Africa, where it is found as far south-east as Madagascar. The plumage is white except for the dark wing-tips and plumes of the lower back; the head and neck are black but are bare of feathers. It usually lives in parties and becomes very tame in places where it is not persecuted.

As the African Yellow-billed Stork (or Wood Ibis) has a very similar Asiatic relative, the Painted Stork, so the African Marabou and the Asiatic Adjutant are very much alike. Although usually called storks, they behave like vultures, feeding on carrion and odd scraps as mentioned above. They wait their turn with vultures, jackals and hyenas while large carnivorous mammals such as lions eat their fill from an antelope or zebra. So long as they do not have to exert themselves too much in the catching of it, they are by no means averse to taking living prey, and have developed the habit of feeding on sickly young flamingos, often those with broken legs or wings, which eke out a miserable existence in the shallows of East African lakes. At Lake Nakuru in Kenya, I have watched Marabou Storks which have learnt to fly over the vast flocks of Lesser Flamingos and, suddenly landing among the densely packed birds, to seize a healthy adult and break its neck before it has a chance to escape.

Most storks have the habit, at times, of perching on the flimsiest tops of trees where they look ungainly and out of place. However, they have learnt to make use of a mechanical principle which gives them stability in this situation: they grasp the 'knee' (in reality the ankle) of one leg with the toes of another, thus forming a triangle, than which nothing could be firmer.

Although many may never actually have seen a flamingo, no one can be unfamiliar with them. They are extraordinary birds, a curious mixture of grotesqueness and almost unbelievable grace. They have a small body suspended, as it were, between disproportionately tall legs and long sinuous necks surmounted by a tiny head, from which protrudes a down-bent bill, the very caricature of a bibulous nose. Their method of feeding is equally curious, the bill being held *upside down* in the water, from which flamingos seldom move very far. The curiously shaped bill is designed to act as a filter: water or sometimes fluid mud is sucked in and the food, almost entirely minute algae and diatoms, is filtered out by a mass of fine 'hairs' and swallowed. In many places where flamingos live the water must be almost totally separated from the food which it contains because to swallow much of it would be dangerous in view of the high concentration of soda or salt in it. Flamingos are found in both the Old and New Worlds, and different species breed from sea level in brackish water to 14,000 feet in the alkaline lakes of the Andes. They breed in colonies, sometimes in huge numbers. Small nests are built, usually of mud, but in the absence of mud of a suitable consistency sometimes gravel, vegetation and feathers are used. Flamingos usually lay only one egg (fewer than one in a hundred nests have two) and the young remain in the nest for a few days after hatching. Later they gather into vast herds within which, incredibly enough, the parents seem able to recognize their own young when they come to feed them. They are grey or greyish-brown at first, but all adult flamingos have some red in their plumage, varying in the different species from white with a pink flush to strong pinkish-red with black wing-tips. They are strong fliers and a large flock in flight vies in its almost unbelievable beauty with one of Scarlet Ibises, already mentioned.

The two species most likely to be seen in the tropics, except by the most travelled and intrepid bird-watcher, are the Lesser and Greater Flamingos each of which is to be found in both Africa and Asia. The Greater, in fact, extends well north of the tropics, with some individuals breeding in southern Europe, and it also inhabits the Bahamas and some parts of South America. The Lesser is by far the most numerous, over two-thirds of the world's flamingos being of this species. On one or two East African lakes it is sometimes possible to see flocks of over one million birds, chiefly Lessers but with a few Greaters among them. These huge flocks have been described as 'the most wonderful ornithological spectacle in the world', and it is indeed difficult to imagine anything more superb. A quite extraordinary sight is the Lesser Flamingo's 'parade' or pre-breeding march, in which hundreds and sometimes thousands of birds join, becoming ever more closely packed together, and, as if at words of command, move as one unit rapidly in one direction, only to halt and as suddenly return. It is amazing how a mass of these birds, each of which looks only faintly pinkish when alone, looks ever deeper and deeper pink as the birds pack close together. It is thought that the redder the colour the greater becomes the stimulation to breed. Most species of flamingo are erratic in their breeding and do not do so by any means every year; they are equally unpredictable in their choice of site, some localities being deserted for a number of years only to be unaccountably re-colonized later.

Waterfowl deserve a book to themselves and it is only possible in a book such as this to deal with them briefly and to select one or two species from each of the tropical zones. Although the word 'waterfowl' is often used to include only ducks (and may even be restricted to those kept in captivity) it is a vague expression and geese and swans may be included under this heading.

In the northern part of its range the Black Swan extends well into the tropics since it occurs in all but the most northerly extremities of Australia. It takes the place in that continent of the Mute Swan which is common in Britain. It is found on quite small fresh-water lakes adjacent to civilization and on larger, more remote waters. When on the water or at rest its plumage appears to be all-black with a bright red bill, but in flight it shows dramatically its white primary wing feathers and becomes most unexpectedly a black and white bird. Like other swans it builds near or in the water a bulky nest of vegetation, and lays from five to ten eggs. The cygnets are light grey at first and are often carried on the parents' backs when on the water. The black plumage is not assumed until they are about a year old.

Two tropical geese which deserve to be mentioned are the Egyptian Goose, which is widespread in Africa, and the Néné or Hawaiian Goose which is as rare as the Egyptian is common. The latter may be seen near water in most of the African National Parks and reserves, especially those in the Rift Valley, but one does not have to travel to Africa to find them since they have for many years been breeding wild in Britain, having escaped or been liberated from captivity. In Norfolk, near Wells and on the Broads, are favourite places. As the breeding season approaches they become very jealous of their chosen territory which is defended against interlopers in most vicious battles. Like the Sacred Ibis, this goose was venerated by the Ancient Egyptians.

The Hawaiian Goose is the subject of what must certainly be regarded as the most successful story of bird conservation so far. This goose was common on two tropical islands, Hawaii and Maui, until the advent of firearms and the introduction of predators such as the mongoose, cat, dog and rat; at about the same time spreading sugar-cane plantations and grazing flocks of sheep and goats began drastically to reduce its breeding habitat. From an estimated 25,000 birds its numbers in the wild had dropped in 1950 to only thirty-five, making, one would have thought, any hope of recovery vain indeed. However, it is a species which is ready to breed in captivity and most fortunately a local property-owner, seeing the species disappearing, had been keeping a breeding stock of Nénés on his land. Both in Hawaii and at the Wildfowl Trust in

*Above* Dissimilar in looks and habits from most birds of prey, the long-legged **Secretary Bird** of the plains of Africa walks around in the grass searching for small reptiles, mice and large insects, which it disturbs with its curious mincing gait. Although it is probably correct to ascribe its name to the resemblance of its head adornments to quill pens stuffed behind its ears, one wonders to what extent the name was also a rather slighting reference to its affected-looking walk.

*Right* One of the most beautiful of an elegant and graceful family, the **Crowned Crane** is rather unusual in quite frequently perching on the tops of trees, which its relations seldom do. Out of the breeding season most cranes can be seen in large flocks, and their wild clanging calls are one of the most thrilling sounds in nature. Sad to say several species are on the danger list and coming perilously close to extinction.

England great efforts were made to establish the birds by breeding from one or two pairs lent by their far-sighted Hawaiian owner. After disappointments and setbacks the project became successful beyond anyone's most optimistic estimates, with the result that captive-bred birds are being released on both Maui and Hawaii and, despite the continued presence and depredations of many of their enemies, the future of the species in the wild seems for the present secure.

Close relatives of the swans and geese are the whistling or tree ducks, of which a good example is the White-faced Tree Duck which is found in tropical South America and Africa. They are poorly named 'tree' ducks because they do not very commonly perch in trees (although a few nest in holes in trees), but their stance on the ground is bold and upright.

The Garganey (often called the Garganey Teal) and the Shoveler are two ducks which merit the name of 'birds of the tropics' because, although they breed in the northern hemisphere, they migrate south when the weather turns colder, huge numbers wintering in Africa and India.

The Garganey is a small duck, the male being beautifully marked in different shades of grey and brown with a most conspicuous white eye-stripe. The Shoveler is large and by comparison a brightly coloured bird, being chestnut, green and white; its large spatulate bill is unmistakable. The females of both are rather dull-coloured, mottled, brown birds. During the peak of migration Shovelers arrive on some north and central Indian waters in immense numbers, and I have seen them on a lake near Delhi so tightly packed that late arrivals were landing on the backs of others because of the lack of open water.

The smallest of the tropical African ducks is the Hottentot Teal, a neat little blue-billed duck with conspicuous white cheeks and a black or very dark brown cap which reaches down to the eye. The back is brown and its breast and underparts are white, prettily speckled with brown.

# Birds of Prey

A bird of prey is usually defined as one which hunts and kills other animals for food, especially vertebrate animals. Thus it is reasonable to include the owls, although they are not so closely related to the true birds of prey as are the vultures, which hardly seem to merit inclusion because they seldom catch live prey except domestic animals, but live mainly on carrion.

In scientific order the New World vultures come first among the birds of prey. It is rather confusing that the most common one, the American Black Vulture, is often called the Buzzard in that country, although it is only a distant relative of the birds more usually known by that name, and it is not even closely related to the Black Vultures of the Old World. Black Vultures are widespread in America and are much persecuted as pests in many places, because they have a reputation for attacking young domestic animals, but in the more backward areas of tropical Central America they serve a very useful purpose as scavengers, not only picking clean the carcasses of animals which have died, but eating almost any filth in open sewers and rubbish dumps, thus keeping down flies and disease.

Two of the New World vultures may be considered tropical birds, the King Vulture and the Condor, which is the largest bird of prey in the world. The former suffers from the same confusion as the Black Vulture, because there is a completely different King Vulture in Asia and, to make the confusion worse, this is also called the Black Vulture and sometimes the Pondicherry Vulture.

The American King Vulture is a remarkable looking bird, with black and white plumage and a naked purplish head with blue cheeks, a grotesque red bill and the most startling black and white eyes surrounded by a red ring. It has a bare red and yellow neck, with a sac which can be inflated during courtship or when excited. It is chiefly a bird of the tropical rain forests, from which it ranges to semi-wooded country and even to open grassland. Although a carrion-eater, it does not associate with man as a cleaner and scavenger, but it is partial to new-born kids and calves and in fact seems to catch rather more live food, such as small reptiles, than do most vultures.

The Osprey comes between the New World vultures and the hawks, and it may come as a surprise to many to find it included as a tropical bird, because it is so closely associated in people's minds with Scotland, where its recent re-establishment is a thrilling story of painstaking protection, and with New York, where until recently there was a huge colony nesting off Long Island. It is however, with the exception of the Peregrine Falcon, the most widely distributed of the world's birds of prey, not only breeding across North America and Europe to the eastern extremity of China, but also in each of the four division of the tropics. It is absent as a breeder from the mainland of South America, but even here it is a regular winter visitor. In the more northerly parts of its range it is a summer visitor, moving south for the winter. Thus in winter in some places, for example lakes almost on the Equator in East Africa, both residents and winter visitors may be seen.

*Top* Bustards, because of their large size and desirability for the pot, are in most cases becoming greatly reduced in numbers, some species appearing doomed to extinction before long. The species most likely to be seen by visitors to the tropics — perhaps to anywhere in the world — is the stately **Kori Bustard** in tropical Africa.

*Above* The **Sunbittern** is a shy bird which lives on the wooded margins of streams in Central and South America, feeding on the numerous small creatures to be found there. It moves very slowly and sedately, stalking its prey with infinite care, head drawn back on its shoulders until the moment when, having reached striking distance, it darts its pointed bill forward on its long thin neck. Sunbitterns have a remarkable dancing display, the male sometimes appearing almost to stand on his head as he points his tail in the air.

The Osprey is almost entirely a fish-eater, although in hard weather small birds or mammals may be taken, and thus it is closely associated with water, both fresh and the sea. It nests in trees, on cliffs, rocks and even buildings and telegraph posts. Surprisingly, although a typical site is a tall pine tree overlooking a lake or a precipitous rock jutting out of the sea, some nests are a considerable distance from water, necessitating a long flight to and from the nest.

It is a wonderful sight to watch an Osprey fishing: it flies with slow, measured flaps over the water, sometimes gliding, sometimes pausing to hover, sometimes rising to circle back over an area in which it may have seen prey, until, sighting a fish close to the surface, it hovers momentarily and then with outstretched feet plunges into the water. On rising – which it may have difficulty in doing if its prey is heavy – it flies for a short distance close above the water, and then, having paused to shake itself rather like a wet dog, it carries its capture to a nearby tree or rock to eat it, or to its nest if it has a sitting mate or youngsters. Both sexes share in incubating the eggs and both feed the chicks.

One of the most beautiful of all birds of prey, the Black-shouldered Kite (sometimes called the Black-winged Kite), is also widespread and is found in all four of the tropical zones. It also extends as far north as the southern part of Portugal where the very few pairs which breed make it one of Europe's rarest breeding birds. It is about the same size as a Kestrel, though rather plumper and with a shorter tail. It is predominantly white, with soft blue-grey back and wings and black 'shoulder-patch'. The white tail is slightly forked and the coloration of its wings gives it a striking black and white appearance when seen from below, since the primaries are grey above and black beneath. It has large, most beautiful, orange-red eyes. They are large because they are adapted to assist in hunting at twilight, which is when the bird often seeks its prey of mice and large insects. The Black-shouldered Kite is interesting in that it is a species which, over its wide range, has adapted itself to breed in widely differing situations, unlike those birds whose distribution is controlled by the existence of suitable sites of a limited type. In savanna and orchard country it will nest in a large bush at a height of no more than ten feet from the ground; where there are tall trees it may build over fifty feet up; in places where there are no suitable trees, it regularly nests on ledges in caves; and in some places it uses the discarded nests of other birds.

The word 'kite' does not at all suit this most attractive, dainty little hawk. Superficially resembling a falcon, it has a mastery of the air equalled by very few, now hovering, now soaring to great heights on motionless outspread wings. Few are likely to see this lovely bird in Europe, but visitors to Africa 'on safari', to India to 'do' the Taj Mahal, or just visiting relations in Australia, should look for it on its favourite perch – the telegraph wires alongside the roads.

A tropical bird of prey which few are likely to see, but which must be mentioned because of its unusual feeding habits, is the Everglade Kite. This feeds almost exclusively on water-snails and thus is confined to fresh-water marshes or areas where there are extensive drainage ditches where these snails live. The male is a lovely shade of grey all over, with brilliant red legs and feet; the female and immature birds are brown. This species is only found in the New World and, although still numerous in South America, it is becoming very rare in its previous tropical North American haunts and is almost certainly on its way to extinction there.

Although absent from America, the Black Kite has a very wide distribution over the rest of the world. It breeds right across Eurasia from the extreme west to Japan, in Africa except for the most arid deserts, in New Guinea and in North Australia. It is not only widespread, but is very common in many of the places where it does occur. Although found in many kinds of habitat, it is partial to the haunts of man and is a useful scavenger right inside many towns in India and Africa, where it breeds in roadside trees. Over some tropical towns the sky sometimes seems full of the tiny dots which are soaring Black Kites, while at the same time others are wheeling in the streets. It is catholic in its feeding habits, eating not only human refuse and carrion but also sickly or dead fish in rivers and lakes, and it is quite expert in catching living prey such as rabbits, rats, young birds, snakes, lizards and large insects such as locusts. It has a wonderfully controlled flight and can wheel and turn in very small places: probably no bird gives a better demonstration of the use of the tail in guiding its direction and elevation. Its call is a distinctive rather querulous

*Above* **Purple Gallinules** are to be found almost all over the world, closely-related species occurring in America, Asia, Africa, Australia, New Zealand and even the south of Europe. They are among the few birds which hold their food up to their bill in one foot. They feed largely on aquatic vegetation, and are very fond of waterlily buds.

*Right* The African **Jacana** is also appropriately called the Lily-trotter from its ability to walk on floating vegetation in what appears to be a most precarious fashion. It is able to do this because of its enormously long toes which spread its weight over a wide area. Although still widespread, it is endangered in some places by the increasing use of high-powered motorboats, the wash from which tips the eggs out of its nest placed on waterlily leaves and other floating plants.

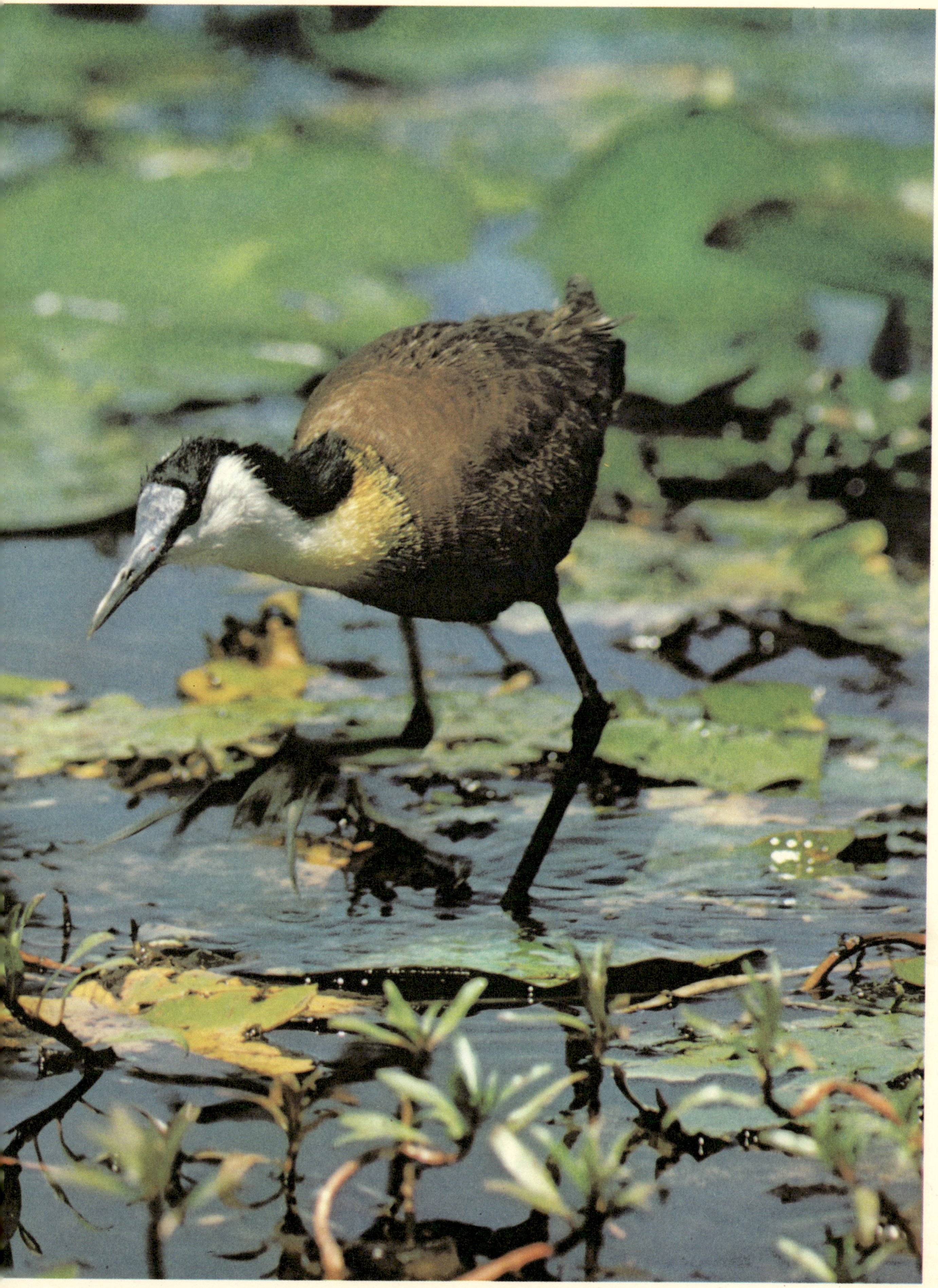

mew or whinnying squeal. Although Black Kites vary in colour throughout their range nowhere are they really black but various shades of brown – usually a rather dark brown. Birds from the north-western part of the species' range have light-coloured heads while those from Africa have the head the same colour as the back and wings.

The African Fish Eagle is confined not only to Africa but to the tropics, except where its range extends south of the Tropic of Capricorn into South Africa. Of all eagles it is the species most likely to be seen by the ordinary tourist who is not an ornithologist in search of rarities, since in tropical Africa it is hardly possible to spend any time near a lake or large river, or for that matter the sea, without seeing – and more especially hearing – it. Of all eagles it is also the most beautiful. The head, breast, back and tail are pure white, while there is chocolate (in some lights rich rufous chestnut) on the belly, shoulders and wings, which also have black in them. In adults the bare skin of the face is brilliant yellow. The bird draws attention to itself by its frequently repeated far-carrying call, which has been variously described as a wild yelp and a yodel. Not only is this often answered by the bird's mate, but the calling of one pair may start others within earshot until, in heavily populated places, the whole area seems to be full of their ringing cries. When calling, the birds throw their heads back in seeming abandon, and they do this even in flight.

Fish Eagles spend much of their time sitting motionless – except for the occasional burst of calling – on trees near or in the water, and do not seem to have to spend much time hunting for their prey. Suddenly one which has been quietly preening will launch itself from its perch and, gliding down to the water, seize in one foot a fish from near the surface. This of course does not apply where fish are scarce or not present at all. In such places the Fish Eagle will catch birds (even flamingos are readily taken in some places) or will chase other birds to rob them of their prey, and it is not averse, when necessary, to eating carrion.

This species builds a large, rather clumsy nest in a tree either near or in the water, and in much of its range it has no set breeding season, sometimes rearing two families in a year, sometimes not nesting at all for two or three years.

The Egyptian Vulture – often called Pharoah's Chicken – is one of the smallest of the vultures and is common in the tropics from India westwards across to the west coast of Africa. In its soaring effortless flight the adult looks most handsome in its apparently black and white plumage, but on the ground, or close to it, it reveals itself as a shaggy, unkempt looking bird, with small head and weak bill and plumage which never looks really clean. The white is in fact tinted with varying degrees of fawn, while immature birds may still have more than traces of the juvenile black or dark brown. As a species it has one very special claim to fame in that, although chiefly a feeder on the filthiest garbage and carrion, it has learnt to steal eggs as large as those of an Ostrich and crack them open by picking up and casting stones on to them, often taking up to a dozen 'shots' at an egg before succeeding in breaking it.

Both Africa and India have their White-backed Vultures and these very closely related species demonstrate well the typical vulturine method of finding food. For hours at a time they will soar on thermals with motionless spread wings, circling slowly and allowing themselves to be drifted gradually across a wide area of country, ever on the lookout for food, usually a dead or dying animal. Their power of sight must be prodigious because they not only scan the ground from a tremendous height but, apparently for many miles around, each vulture is keeping its eyes upon its fellows so that, if one shows signs of having found a carcass by planing down to investigate, another and yet another will follow suit until vultures are gathering from great distances to join in the feast. As the first ones are satiated and withdraw to recover (I have seen them when they had gorged so much that they could not fly) others are descending from the heavens to take their place, until there are sometimes literally hundreds of vultures around one quickly disappearing carcass. In Africa the food is usually the remains of the kill of large predators such as lions, and while the rightful owners are still feeding the vultures keep at a respectful distance, but when all is clear the White-backed are among the first to claim priority. However, even they may have to give way if a large Lappet-faced Vulture or Marabou Stork is present, and later they in their turn will make room for the weak Hooded and Egyptian Vultures which wait on the outskirts of the jostling fighting mob for the scraps which are left.

In India, where unfortunately mammalian predators have been almost exterminated, the carcass is probably that of a poor underfed and overworked domestic cow or camel, and usually the Whitebacked Vultures' only competitors are dogs, although in the less-populated areas jackals and hyenas may try to take a share. A large dog may hold the vultures at bay while he eats, but more often dogs and vultures share the feast, though not without a great deal of bickering.

Although vultures may appear by our standards to have disgusting habits and their bare heads and scrawny necks are anything but beautiful to look at, there is no doubt at all that some countries, notably India with its large human population, owe them a great debt as scavengers and preventers of disease, and no birds are more wonderful in their powers of soaring flight.

The Galapagos Hawk, which might better be called a buzzard, is confined to the Galapagos Islands, and has become one of the world's rarest birds of prey because of persecution by man. Like all the wild creatures of these islands they are remarkably tame and were easily killed when raiding chicken-runs. It is to be hoped that they are safer now that the Galapagos Islands are rated as a National Park. The adult birds are a dark brownish-black all over, but in immature plumage they might easily be mistaken for Common Buzzards since they are lighter brown with pale speckled underparts.

Galapagos Hawks live on a wide range of foods, from small reptiles, insects and the young of sea birds to carrion. A rather bulky nest of sticks and twigs is built, usually in a rocky site, and the young stay with their parents long after they can fend for themselves. The species has in fact unusually gregarious habits for a buzzard and in many places a number of families combine to form a community which lives apparently without territorial squabbling, at least for feeding purposes.

Surely no-one with an eye for birds who visits tropical East Africa can fail to see the beautiful Augur Buzzard, a medium-sized black and white bird of prey with a conspicuous chestnut-red tail; at rest there is a patch of black and white bars in the wings. It is so often seen because of its habit of sitting on roadside telegraph poles, which it uses as vantage points from which to pounce on small creatures below. Unfortunately it and the Long-crested Hawk Eagle, another tropical African bird of prey with similar habits, are often killed on the roads by passing cars, and one can see all-too-many of their mangled bodies on the roads around Nairobi.

The Secretary Bird may seem to many people to fit stangely among hawks and eagles, but it is indeed a bird of prey, even if a rather peculiar one. It has a light grey body about the size of a large eagle, with a rather long, thin neck and small head with bare red skin around the eyes. The central tail feathers are greatly elongated and the back of its head is adorned with a crest of 'quills' from which it gets its name. The belly, rump, flight feathers, 'thighs' and bars on the tail are black. Its very long legs and its habit of searching out its prey on the ground by walking along with mincing gait, head bobbing forward with each step and pointing downwards, are distinctive features. It is forever walking, now in a straight line, now circling round, but never apparently in daylight hours at rest unless it is on its nest. It feeds on all manner of ground creatures to be found in the grasslands where it lives, from quite small insects to small mammals, birds and snakes. It builds a large, flat nest on or near the top of a flat-topped bush or small tree, and if this happens to be, as it often is, a thick acacia or 'thorn bush' the nest may be almost impossible to see from the ground unless the bird chances to be standing on it. The young are fed by regurgitation and are tended by both parents. Owing to the fact that the nest is open to the sky, they are very vulnerable to flying predators and infant mortality must be very great. However, the Secretary Bird is still numerous in many parts of its range and is undoubtedly the friend of man, since almost all its food consists of creatures which would be described as noxious or pests.

Tropical Central America has a bird of prey which, although falcon-like in many respects, is much more sluggish than most falcons and certainly lacks the verve of, for example, the Peregrine. The Laughing Falcon, instead of catching its food by a rapid chase ending in a thrilling 'stoop', does so by sitting quite still, often for hours, until a snake or lizard chances to pass beneath the perch on which it is waiting. It then drops silently on to its prey, which it grips behind the head in its bill, thus making it impossible for a counter-attack to take place, which is so necessary in the case of a poisonous snake. Some protection against the bites of these is also provided

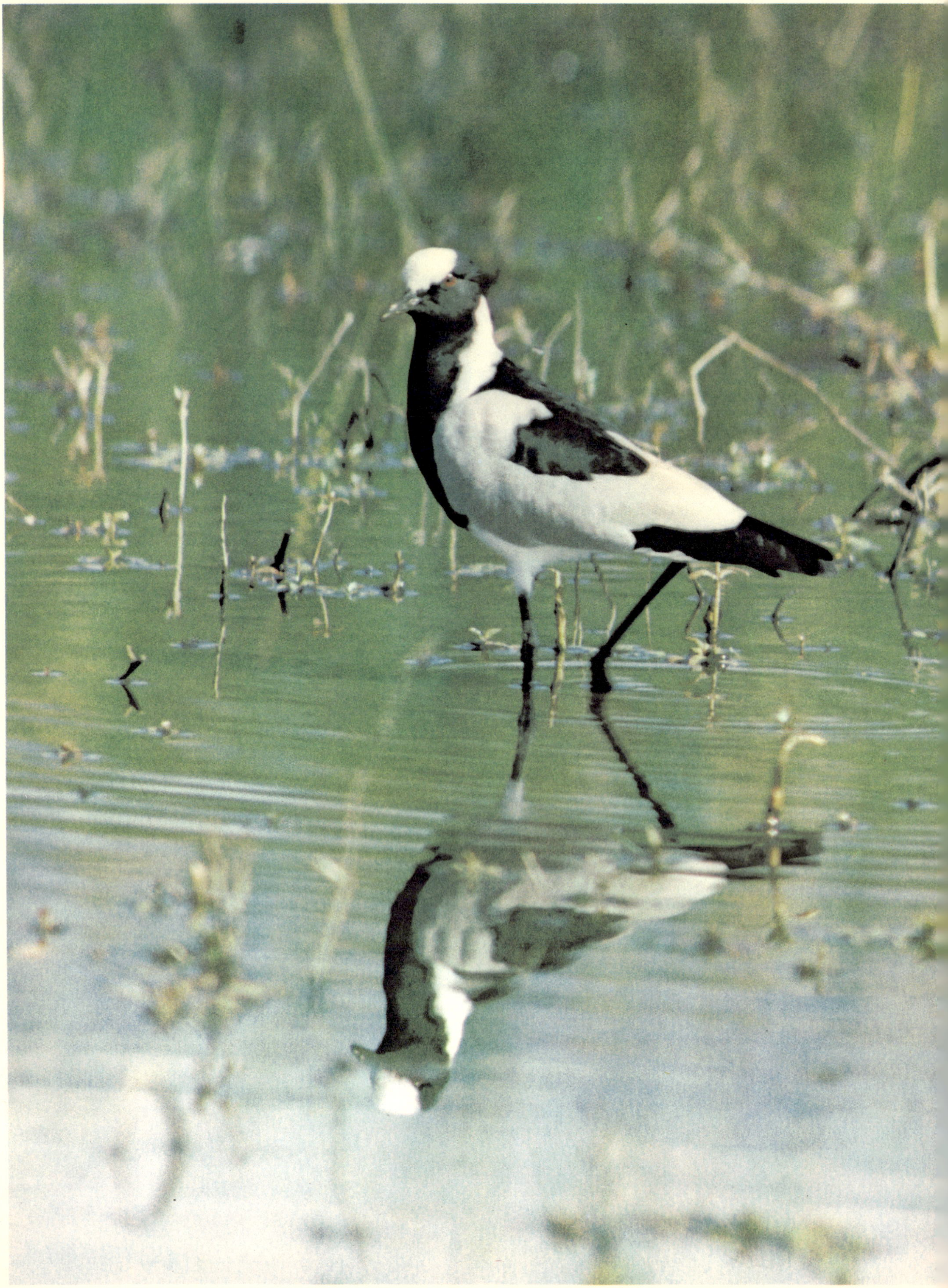

*Left* The **Blacksmith Plover** — a study in black, white and grey greatly enhanced by its gorgeous red eye — is often to be seen in pairs even out of the breeding season, unlike many of its relatives which gather into large flocks. It received its name because its call is said by some people to resemble the hammering of metal upon an anvil.

*Above* The **Red-wattled Lapwing** is a noisy and excitable Asiatic representative of the large plover family, which has the reputation among 'sportsmen' — and even among bird-watchers — of giving other creatures warning of the approach of man. However it helps the bird-photographer, if he does manage to get near to it, by standing still momentarily between its brisk, spasmodic movements.

by the unusually tough scales on the falcon's legs and feet.

The bird gets its name from its alarm call 'Hahahahaha'. Like most falcons, it does not build a nest of its own but lays its egg in the disused nest of another bird or in a hollow or depression in a tree where a branch has broken off. Only one egg is laid and, at any rate while the chick is small, the male bird provides all the food for the family while the female keeps guard at the nest.

Although owls are not generally considered to be tropical birds they do occur in the tropics and a few species deserve to be mentioned. Owls are regarded as nocturnal birds of prey, and it is true that most of them spend their daylight hours hidden in dense foliage or holes in trees and rocks and come out at dusk or during the night to hunt for food. However, some species are habitually about in daylight. The idea that 'owls can see in the dark' is not true – no living creature can see when it is completely dark – although their eyes are so well adapted to using the absolute minimum of light that they can hunt at times when, to human eyes, there is no light at all. They are helped in finding their food, which consists of a variety of living food from insects to fairly large mammals such as hares, and even fish, by exceptionally good hearing and very soft feathers which ensure silent flight. Owls have very flexible necks which enable them to rotate their head in a remarkable way, sometimes more than 270 degrees.

One of the most attractive tropical owls is the African White-faced Scops Owl, which usually lays its eggs in a hole in a tree but may choose the abandoned nest of another bird. Although it mainly feeds on large insects, it will also take mice, rats, lizards and frogs. It is a small owl, between eight and ten inches long. At the other end of the scale is Verreaux's Eagle Owl, the most powerful owl of tropical Africa, being two feet long and with a wing span of at least four feet. It is greyish-brown above, finely marked with buff and grey; the wings and tail are broadly barred with dark brown and white specks. Underneath it is paler and finely barred with grey-brown. An extraordinary feature, the reason for which is unknown, is its pink eyelids which are conspicuous unless the eyes are very widely open. Although its food is principally mammals, such as rats, hares and hedgehogs, it will also take roosting birds, large insects and reptiles.

The Barn Owl has a world-wide distribution and is found in suitable habitats in all parts of the tropics except the North African deserts, west-central Africa and some of the East Indian Islands. It also spreads both north and south of the tropical zone, Scotland being the northern extremity of its range. It is mainly a bird of open country and, in places where it lives near man, it is especially partial to roosting and breeding in buildings, from deserted ruins to barns in daily use, a habitat from which of course it gets its name. In wilder places it uses hollow trees, rock crevices and caves. This is the owl which has given rise to many ghost stories, because it not only appears largely white when in flight, and produces eerie shrieks, but in addition it utters weird snoring noises. Superstitious and nervous people may perhaps be forgiven for their alarm, because claims that the bird is illumined by a ghostly glow have been proved to have some truth, since the birds may have luminous bacteria on their feathers which probably originated in decaying matter in the nest or roosting hole. It is a most valuable ally to man, because it destroys vast numbers of rats and mice.

# Cranes, Gallinules and Bustards

On the ground, whether standing or walking, no birds are more stately than cranes, while their flight – with its slow measured wing-beats, the up-stroke looking faster than the down – is a thrilling sight, especially when a flock is flying high up, in V-formation, the individuals keeping in touch by their wild, trumpeting clarion-call. They are conspicuous birds and stand and walk with their necks upstretched and alert, except when feeding or leaving their nest.

Out of the breeding season cranes are gregarious birds, often gathering in large flocks at their winter feeding grounds. All species have the extraordinary habit, before breaking up into pairs for nesting, of indulging in a communal dancing ceremony, which in some species is continued – usually in a more subdued manner – when a pair has mated and begun nesting. Although these dances vary in their pattern somewhat from species to species and perhaps according to the season, they often include what may be described as a rather formal 'quick-step'. The birds walk stiffly round and round, now and then bowing to each other, sometimes looking remarkably as though they were elegant ladies and gentlemen 'treading a measure'; or they may leap high in the air, on landing to throw their heads backwards, sometimes so far as to touch their back with the crown of their head. They may pick up anything which happens to be on the ground, such as a stick, and throw it into the air, sometimes stabbing at it or appearing to try to catch it as it descends. Although, as has been said, a form of this dance may be performed near the nest by a mated pair (for example by the so-called 'Common' Crane, which breeds in the far north and is a bird of the tropics only in the European winter), it tends to be more intense and enthusiastic as the number of birds taking part increases, and it seems to be by no means purely related to courtship or sex. It may be seen among immature birds as well as adults and it is difficult to escape the impression that, in part at least, it is an expression of high spirits. Whatever its main purpose, there can be little doubt that it serves as a link between members of the flock. Although the very nature of this display usually calls for it to be performed on the ground, African Crowned Cranes have been seen to 'dance' while perched on the top of a tall tree.

All species of crane nest on the ground, usually in wild or remote places (although the Crowned Crane has occasionally been found nesting on the flat top of a bush or even a tree), the nest itself varying from a mere flattening of a circle of grass to a substantial mound of reeds or whatever vegetation is to hand. Many nests are built in inaccessibly marshy places, probably as a protection against predators, and the size of the nest is often related to the wetness of the surrounding terrain. The eggs, usually two only, range from dull white or bluish-white or brown, spotted and blotched with darker brown, according to the species. Both sexes share the incubation, as they do nest-building and tending the young. Since incubation (which lasts a month or five weeks) begins when the first egg is laid, and there is usually an interval of forty-eight hours between laying, one egg tends

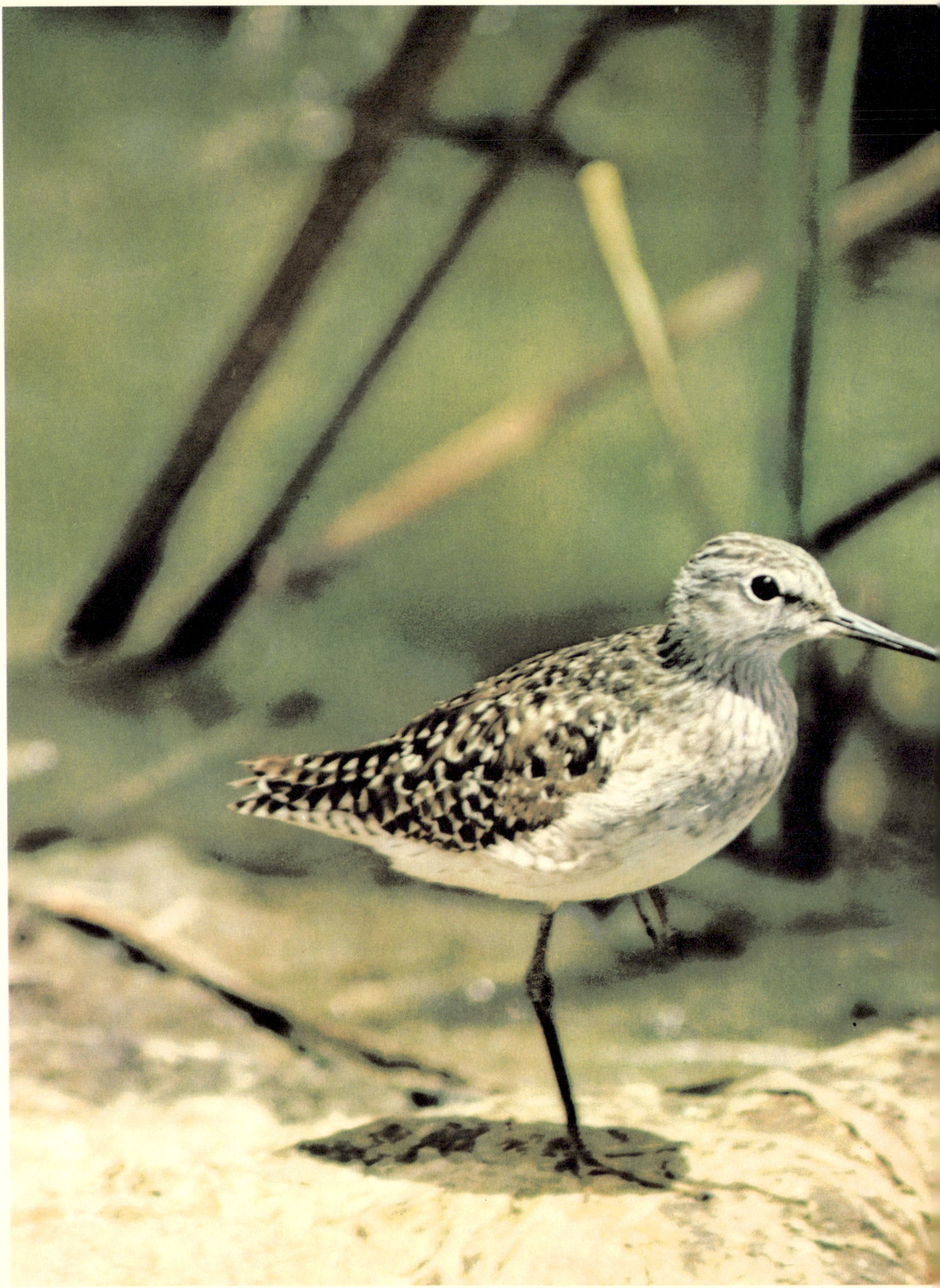

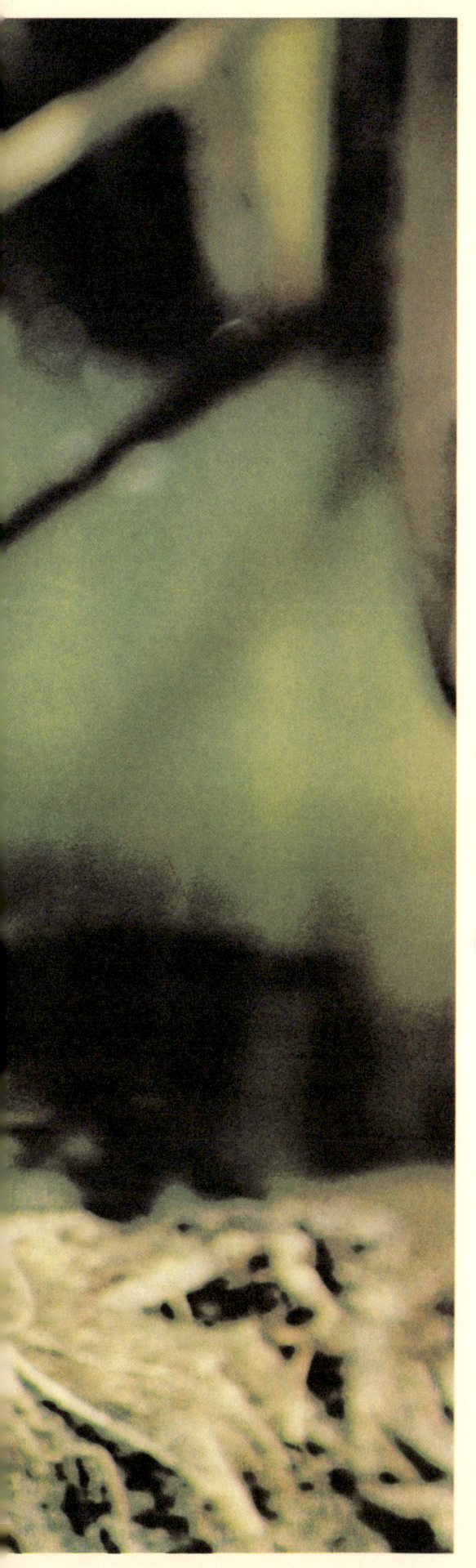

*Left* This **Wood Sandpiper**, photographed in February almost on the equator in Africa, had flown all the way from its breeding haunts in the north (probably Scandinavia) in order to avoid the harsh winter. Most sandpipers lay their eggs on the ground, making little or no nest though sometimes drawing growing vegetation over themselves as they sit. The Wood Sandpiper is no exception, and in the north it frequently lays its eggs on reindeer moss, where their coloration makes them all but invisible.

*Top* Sandgrouse are relatives of the pigeons, but inhabit dry, sandy, open country. Because of their normally arid habitat, which makes frequent drinking impossible, they have developed the habit of drinking morning or evening, often flying considerable distances to favourite streams or water-holes to do so. They are so faithful to these drinking places and so regular in the time of their arrival that they fall easy prey to both hunters and animal predators, and it is wonderful that a bird which does not appear to rear a very large number of young each year is able to keep up its numbers. The **Blackfaced Sandgrouse** illustrated is found from Somaliland southwards to Tanzania.

*Above* Bird-seed thrown down had attracted this **Spotted Dove** to a garden in India.

Although the words 'pigeon' and 'dove' are popularly believed to apply to large and small members of this very large family (there are nearly 300 species) this is not in any way a scientific distinction and in some cases both words are used as alternative names for the same bird: for example Wood Pigeon and Ring Dove are the same species.

Pigeons vary greatly in size, from the little Australian Diamond Dove, not much larger than a sparrow with a long tail, to the Crowned Pigeon of New Guinea which is as large as a goose. Most species are vegetarians, but some take small creatures such as snails, worms and insects.

to hatch some time before the other. Cranes can walk and even swim very soon after hatching, and the parent which is not engaged in incubation takes charge of the first-born and often leads it a considerable distance from the nest to feed, although it is usually brought back at night to be brooded, at any rate for the first few days. Young cranes are noisy while still in the egg and while photographing cranes at their nest in a Norwegian mountain marsh, I was able to hear them clearly giving a very juvenile version of the trumpet call from inside the unhatched eggs, from my hide thirty feet away.

The parents encourage the young to feed by holding in front of them in their own bill small pieces of food which they have picked up. Cranes eat both vegetable and animal matter – roots, berries, insects and mice – and feed in many types of open country from marshes to dry savanna, and may commonly be seen on cultivated land provided that they are not persecuted. Some species, like the Cattle Egret, have the habit of attending browsing cattle to catch the small creatures which they disturb, while on the other hand the African Crowned Crane, although it has just as varied a diet as most other species, is often to be seen walking through tall grass nipping off the seed heads.

Although their numbers have been sadly depleted during the last hundred or so years and the very existence of some species is threatened, cranes are found in most parts of the world except South America, New Zealand and the islands of the Pacific. Their large size and habit of gathering in large parties makes them very vulnerable both to 'sportsmen' and to those anxious for easily-gained food. Even one of the rarest species of all, the Siberian White Crane, is to be seen hanging up for sale in the markets in some parts of India. But it is not only direct persecution which is reducing the numbers of many species; as is the case of so many wild creatures, man's destruction of their habitat is the most potent cause of their rapid decline and few, if any, species of crane are escaping this. Fortunately they have a degree of protection in some countries, such as from the religious beliefs and superstition of the Buddhists, and from sentiment – never to be sneered at – in places so far apart as Sweden and Japan, quite apart from reserves and conservation efforts in many parts of the world.

There are fourteen (possibly fifteen) species of crane, widely distributed, of which two of the best known species – probably because they are among the most frequently kept in zoos – are the Sarus and the Crowned Crane. The latter is restricted to Africa, but the Sarus Crane has a wide range, which it seems to be extending, from West Pakistan, across India, Burma and Thailand down towards Australia, where it is now reported to be breeding in small numbers.

One of the largest and most stately of cranes, it is a silvery, bluish-grey bird with darker greyish-brown wings and red head and upper neck, apart from the crown and forehead which are a very light grey. As in other species, the secondary feathers are elongated to form plumes looking like a drooping bushy 'tail', and these in the Sarus Crane are such a light grey as to appear white in some lights. The red on the head is bare skin, not feathers. The young are covered with greyish-brown down when first hatched and they take nearly three months to reach the flying stage.

Although obviously from the same family, the African Crowned Crane is a very different bird from the Sarus. It is much smaller, and in place of the overall sober grey of the latter it has black and white wings shading into gold behind with rich chestnut-red secondaries, a black head with pure white patches behind the eye, a brilliant red wattle below the chin, a rich blue-grey back and, literally 'to crown all', a tufted golden topknot which stands stiffly erect like a spread brush. As if this were not enough the feathers of the neck and back are plume-like and droop gracefully down over the rest of the body.

The nesting habits are very similar to those described for other cranes and it performs equally – perhaps even more – elaborate dances. Considering that it is a lighter bird than some, its flight appears curiously heavy and more laboured than that of its relatives; this impression is probably heightened by the fact that in flight it holds its neck in a downward curve with the head lower than the back, while the legs droop at an angle behind. This is, however, misleading since in reality it is a strong flier and needs a shorter 'take-off run' than its heavier cousins.

Most species of crane do well in captivity and very few zoological gardens are without a few examples. Some will breed fairly freely but it is to be hoped that the welcome spread of realization of the need for conservation of wildlife means that it will continue to be possible for many years to enjoy the sight of them in the freedom of their natural habitat.

Near to the cranes in the scientific order of species come the rails and gallinules. These are small to bantam-sized birds which live on the ground, often in wet places, and many species inhabit dense vegetation. Most species walk with bobbing head and flirting tail, and those which habitually swim do so with the same jerky movement of the head. Some of them are strong fliers but many of those which live on remote islands have lost some of their power of flight and are an easy prey for introduced predators such as rats, with the result that of the 130 or more species which are known about ten are already extinct.

Some species are largely vegetarian in their diet; others prefer animal food or a mixture of both, and are not above taking the small young of other species; quite a few are nocturnal and are difficult to see and study, so that much of their life-history is unrecorded. Some are very noisy, making sounds which range from clucks and pops to loud squeals. All species tend to conceal their nests carefully – some are very difficult indeed to find – and they lay rather large clutches of eggs, sometimes up to a dozen or more. Usually both sexes share in incubation and tending the down-covered young, which usually leave the nest soon after hatching and can immediately walk and swim.

Almost everyone must be familiar with moorhens and coots, but most of the rails and crakes are rather skulking, seldom-seen birds which live in reed-beds or thick low vegetation. Whilst many of these are not likely to show themselves, except by the purest chance, to any but the most ardent bird-watcher, the Purple Gallinule is a bird which visitors to lakes in the parts of the world which they inhabit can scarcely miss. It is especially easily seen in the reserves of East Africa and north-central India, although curiously enough its close relations in southern Europe are not so obliging and are rather secretive birds, while on the other side of the world there are some roadside lakes in Australia where they are very approachable, though these are rather outside the scope of this book.

The Purple Gallinule is strikingly coloured in blue, purple and blue-green (rather depending on the light), with bright red or yellow legs, according to the part of the world, and red 'frontal shield' extending back over the forehead. The Purple Gallinules of the New World have a greyish coloured shield while the Indian ones have a grey head but a red shield. All have very long toes adapted for walking on floating vegetation and for grasping buds and roots and holding them up to be eaten.

Although not closely related, the bustards come near to the rails and coots in scientific order. They are medium- to very-large-sized birds and live mainly in dry, grassy plains and deserts; most are strong fliers, but they spend the majority of their time on the ground, preferring to use their powerful legs rather than their wings. On the approach of danger some species tend to crouch motionless instead of running away, and their mainly brown or grey plumage is well adapted to concealment. They eat both animal and vegetable matter.

In some bustards the male is larger than the female (sometimes considerably so) and at the beginning of the breeding season he performs a most extraordinary display. This has been described as 'turning himself inside out' and, so much does he contort himself, that it is often momentarily impossible to tell which is head and which is tail. The effect of this, which completely changes his appearance and in some species briefly makes him appear to be almost entirely white, is most startling and probably serves the dual purpose of warning to other males and 'shock courtship' to watching females. Some species form pairs at nesting time, the male standing guard near the incubating female; others are promiscuous and the males leave nesting and rearing duties entirely to their mates. The blotched brownish eggs are laid in a scrape on the bare ground, with little or no attempt at nest-building, and the young leave the nest soon after hatching.

Bustards are usually wary, unapproachable birds, and the one most likely to be seen by visitors to the tropics is the large Kori Bustard of East and South Africa, although even in the sanctuary of the national parks this has the habit of showing only a back view as it stalks away and rapidly disappears from sight. It is a rather dark brown bird with fawn markings, and has a flat-topped head with a crest at the back and, especially in the male, an unmistakable 'thick' neck. Except when a female is accompanied by one or two chicks, Kori Bustards are usually solitary birds.

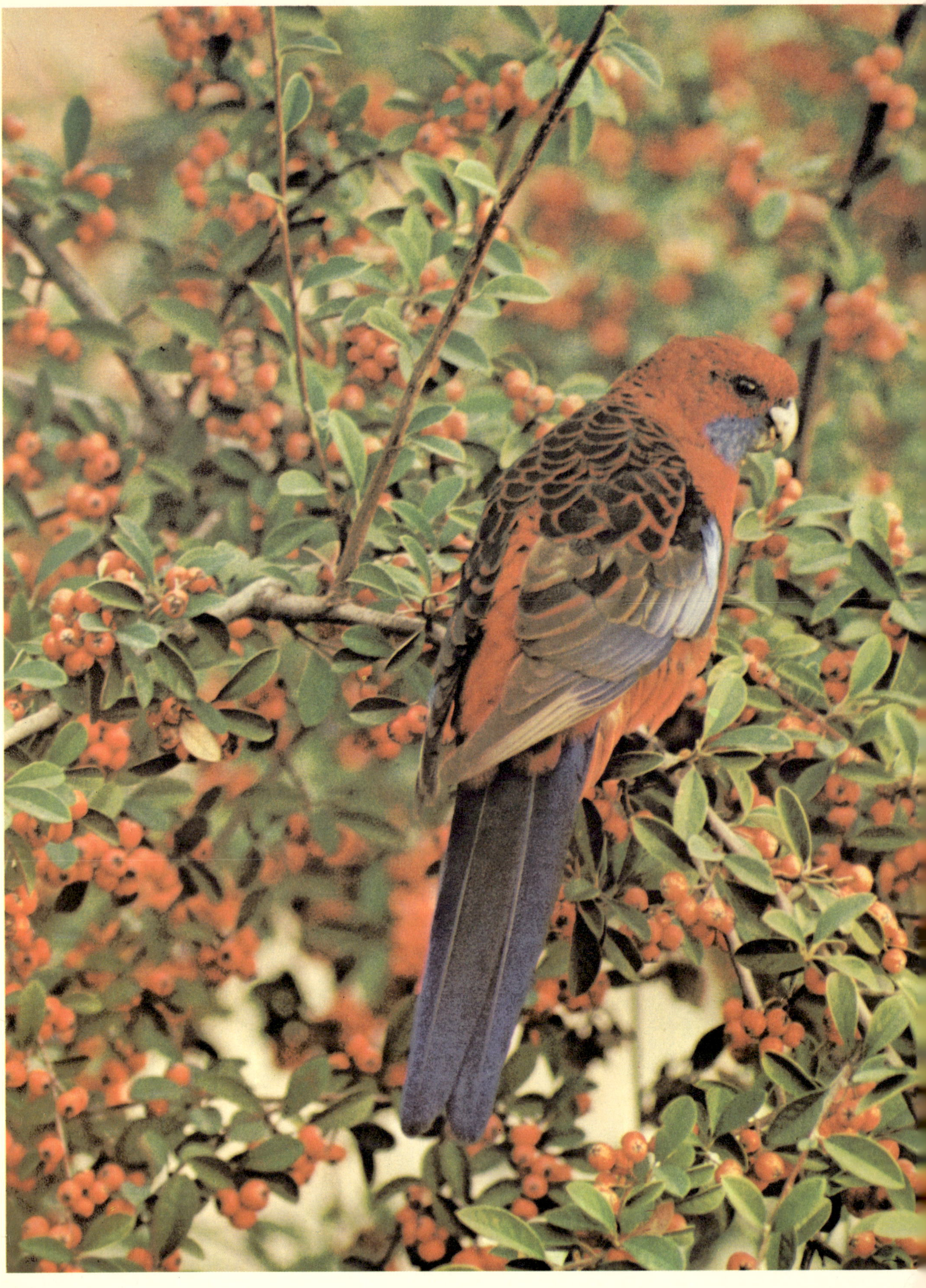

*Left* **Crimson Rosella**. This beautiful parrot was photographed in Australia, where it is found all along the eastern side except the most northern tip. In its native country it is often called the Lowry, and in many parts of the world Pennant's Parrakeet. Although acacia seeds and native fruits are its usual food, in some districts it causes much damage in orchards.

*Above* The reason for the name of the **Ring-Necked Parrakeet** appears obvious until one sees only a female, which has no ring round its neck. These birds inhabit both Africa and India, but are more likely to be seen by the ordinary tourist in the latter, where parties commonly feed on roadside berries and even fly noisily calling through the towns. They nest in holes, chiefly in trees but sometimes in buildings and, like most hole-nesting birds, their eggs are pure white. The young are fed on regurgitated, partly-digested, food by both parents.

Parrakeets are popular aviary birds and many species breed so freely in captivity that they may almost be considered to be domesticated; certainly there is no justification for the trapping and exporting from their native haunts of such species. Fortunately it is illegal to do so in some parts of the world, but unhappily the Ring-necked Parrakeet is trapped in India and nearby countries and exported in thousands, despite the fact that it is not difficult to breed in aviaries. These captives are so badly treated and poorly housed and fed that many — probably the majority — do not survive to become someone's pet.

# Waders, Gulls and Terns

Jacanas, often called lily-trotters or lotus birds, are found on ponds and lakes overgrown with waterlilies and similar plants in almost all parts of the tropics. Different species inhabit Africa, India, south-east Asia, and Indonesia through to northern Australia. They are rail-like birds, most having brown, yellow and white in their plumage and all seven species have in common the remarkably elongated toes which make it possible for them to walk on floating vegetation by spreading their weight over a wide area. One species, the Pheasant-tailed Jacana of Asia, assumes a striking nuptial plumage which includes the very long tail feathers from which it gets its name, and which make it look very different from the rather drab brown and white bird of the non-breeding season.

Lily-trotters eat a wide variety of living matter associated with the water where they live, from insects and tadpoles to aquatic vegetation. They have a characteristic high-stepping gait with a flick of the tail at each stride of their long legs. They are good swimmers and both adults and tiny young remain hidden for considerable periods with little more than their head above water. The nest is built on floating plants and the eggs must spend much time submerged. Four eggs make the normal clutch but many nests have fewer because of losses from such disasters as an unusually high wave or the approach of a heavy-footed creature which causes the nest to tip.

Plovers are medium-sized or smallish birds and many members of the family are more familiarly known as 'lapwings'. There are over fifty species spread over almost all the world, a great many being tropical. One of the most widespread is the Kentish Plover, and it is certainly one of the least aptly named because it is found in all four regions of the tropics but is virtually extinct in Britain.

Plovers are inhabitants of open spaces; they are strong fliers and some species fly immense distances on migration; they feed and spend most of their time on the ground and many species are found near water or in damp or marshy places. The 'nest' of most of them consists of nothing more than a shallow hollow in the bare ground, although some make a rather elementary attempt at nest-building by gathering a few sticks, stones or even rabbit-droppings. Four stone- or olive-coloured eggs covered in black or brown spots and blotches are the rule, but two to five eggs may be laid by some members of the family. The young are nidifugous – that is they leave the nest and are strong on their legs very soon after hatching – and are very difficult to see when they crouch motionless, being coloured to match their surroundings. A few species which habitually nest on sand cover their eggs (they might almost be said to bury them) when they leave them. Both sexes normally share in incubation and caring for the young. Some have delightful little displays when they relieve each other at the nest; the Little Ringed Plover, for example, picks up small pebbles and casts them 'over his shoulder' when near the nest.

Most plovers, especially the large species, have boldly contrasting colours in the plumage, mainly black, white and brown and, because this breaks up their outline

**Renauld's Ground Cuckoo** is a remarkable-looking bird and an observer might well be excused for thinking it a brightly coloured pheasant rather than a cuckoo. In fact it is a relative of the Coucal illustrated on page 52, a bird whose alternative name 'Crow-pheasant' shows that the resemblance is considerable, although pheasants and cuckoos are scientifically very dissimilar.

when they are not moving, they can disappear into their surroundings in a remarkable way even when part of the large flocks into which many species congregate out of the breeding season. The Blacksmith and Crowned Plovers of Africa and the Red-wattled Lapwing of India provide good examples of this type of coloration, even the brilliant red around the face of the last-named being much less conspicuous at a little distance than might be imagined. The Blacksmith is perhaps the most beautiful of all the plovers: clad in sober black, white and grey, its bold carriage and lovely red eyes are unforgettable, especially when reflected in the water as in the illustration on page 38. It is almost certain to be seen by visitors to the Rift Valley lakes in Kenya.

At the other end of the scale is the plainer but quite charming little Kittlitz's Sand Plover which is only about six inches long and is a widespread resident in East and Central Africa, being found both on the coast and around inland waters. It is remarkably fearless and, were it not so small, would be one of the easiest of African waders to photograph because it will often allow a car within a few feet. It has a white forehead band which continues round the back of the neck, forming a white collar, a dark stripe just below the eye, also continuing backwards to the sides of the neck, dark upperparts and paler buff-coloured breast.

Closely related to the plovers are the sandpipers. The Wood Sandpiper is a good example of a bird which winters in the tropics but migrates northwards to breed. It has a wide distribution, in summer from Britain eastwards to the extreme east of Russia, and in winter from Africa across India and Indonesia to Australia. Like many other waders it has the habit of not only standing on one foot to sleep but of hopping, still with one leg tucked up under it, for considerable distances, especially when disturbed while resting. This frequently gives rise to quite unmerited sympathy in the minds of the uninitiated.

Another black and white wader which needs no bright colours to enhance its beauty (although it has red legs) is the Black-winged Stilt, so named because of its very long legs. This is found in all four of our tropical regions and always near or in water, from which it obtains practically all its food. Its long legs enable it to feed in much deeper water than most other waders. It is both sedentary and migratory, but the degree to which it is a truly regular migrant is difficult to determine, because it has the habit of deserting an apparently favoured haunt, only to turn up again years later.

Gulls are known to everyone and are found almost all over the world although, contrary to popular belief, most species are not seen far out at sea. The expression 'sea-gull' is therefore not a very apt one, especially since many of them breed far inland. They are strong fliers and swimmers and most species, though preferring fish, will eat almost anything and they spend much of their time scavenging. Their smaller and more graceful relatives the terns, on the other hand, are usually more particular and eat mainly small fish and other marine animals, while a few which inhabit inland waters are expert fly-catchers. Terns are more slender birds than gulls and have long narrow wings and often forked tails, from which they get their name of 'sea swallows'. The inclusion of three tropical members of this large family must suffice: the Grey-headed Gull of the African lakes, which assumes its pearly-grey head only for the breeding season; the Inca Tern of the west coast of tropical South America, which in plumage colour may lay claim to being the most beautiful member of the family; and the Fairy Tern, more properly called a 'noddy', which is a widespread breeder on the islands of the tropical seas. The Inca Tern is slate-coloured in general plumage with white bands in the wings, white plumes near the eyes, and yellow wattles at the base of the bill which, like the feet, is bright crimson. Unlike most terns, it nests in holes or burrows. The Fairy Tern – a dainty little pure white bird with a black bill – lays a single egg in a most precarious position, such as a flat place on a branch of a tree, its chick being able to cling on with its claws. This bird has the misfortune to have become a tourist attraction at some 'recently-discovered' resorts such as the Seychelle Islands, and will almost certainly suffer as a consequence.

# Parrots

The 300 or more species of parrot range from the tiny pygmy parrots of Papua and New Guinea, which are little more than three inches long, to the forty-inch macaws of South America; and from dumpy, thick-set birds to streamlined ones with long tails. Yet all parrots have so many features in common that there is never any doubt as to which family they belong. All members of this large family have short, stout, down-curved, hooked bills, strong grasping feet with two toes forward and two backward, rather small but bright eyes, large heads and short necks, and all have the power of moving the upper mandible, which is articulated with the skull. All species lay white eggs and the young are hatched naked and helpless, being fed by their parents by regurgitation of partly-digested food.

Nearly all parrots nest in holes, mainly in trees but sometimes among rocks, in sand banks or in termite mounds. One species, however, the Ground Parrot of Australia, nests in tufts of grass, while one South American parrakeet builds huge colonial nests among the branches of trees.

With such a large family of mainly beautifully coloured birds to choose from, it is difficult to know which species most deserve special mention. The Rainbow Lorikeet, distributed from Indonesia and Australia eastwards to the New Hebrides, lives up to its name, having a bright blue head and belly, scarlet chest suffused with yellow at the sides, green back, wings and tail, yellow nape and coral-red bill. Like other lories and lorikeets it has a brush-like tip to its tongue with which it gathers nectar from flowers which are rich in honey. Probably lorikeets play a considerable part in pollination. They also eat berries and buds, and some take insects.

The Palm Cockatoo from the same region – though with a more restricted range – is the largest of the Australasian parrots and is an exception to the general rule of the family in having black plumage instead of the more usual greens, blues and reds. The black is relieved by cheek patches of bare red skin. Cockatoos have erectile crests and the bills of the larger species such as this one (often called the Great Black Cockatoo) are strong enough to crack nuts so hard-shelled that a man would require a hammer. Most cockatoos are gregarious, but the Black is a rather solitary bird, usually keeping to the tops of tall trees either by itself or with only one or two companions.

One of the most colourful of the cockatoos, the Pink or Leadbeater's, is sometimes described, not without good reason, as the most beautiful Australian bird. The back, wings and tail are mainly white, with the inner webs of the primaries, secondaries and inner tail feathers red. The cheeks, chin, breast and sides of the body are a most lovely salmon pink, while the under-wings are a deeper pink and the forehead is rose-red. Each long feather of the crest has a broad deep red band at its lower end, with a large orange-yellow mark on it and then a quite broad white tip. When erected, as it frequently is, its beauty is greatly enhanced by the short outer crest feathers which are pure white.

The macaws of the tropical rain forests of

A **Common Coucal** or **Crow-pheasant** beside an Indian stream. Different species of coucals range across the tropics from Africa through Asia to Australia and as far as the Solomon Islands. Despite their name, they are neither crows nor pheasants but are related to cuckoos.

Only the male **Streamertail Hummingbird** of Jamaica, which is known there as 'the doctor bird', has the long tail feathers. Although seldom far from trees, it is at home in a variety of habitats and has even managed to adapt itself to places where man has completely changed the landscape. To obtain this picture advantage was taken of the bird's habit of repeatedly returning to a favourite perch between sorties after nectar or insects.

Central and South America are the largest of the parrots. Most of them are huge, gaudy birds three feet in length of which the tail takes up nearly two thirds. (The Australian Palm Cockatoo is nearly as large.) Some people would say they are the most beautiful of the parrots, although their reputation for beauty lies mainly in their very bright, sharply contrasting colours which are utterly unlike the delicate tones of Leadbeater's Cockatoo, and comparison can only be a matter of opinion.

Perhaps the best known of all the parrots is the African Grey, because it is the most frequently kept as a house pet and it is a wonderful mimic, thus being famed as 'the best talker', though why anyone should want to teach a bird to utter sounds so unnatural to it as the human voice, especially the remarkably silly things which it is usually taught to say, is beyond comprehension, particularly when it will quite naturally pick up some of the more amusing sounds around it.

It is hardly necessary to say that its main body plumage is grey, lighter on the rump and belly and darker on the wings. The tail is a beautiful deep red. The plumage of its upper head and back has a scaly appearance due to the grey feathers being edged with white or lighter grey. It is distributed over most of tropical Africa but is not easy to see in the tree tops, a hasty glimpse of a party flying high from one patch of cover to the next being all that many visitors to its haunts will get. It sometimes does much damage to crops.

The Ring-necked Parrakeet is found in Africa and Asia, and the slightly larger Asian one is often known as the Rose-ringed Parrakeet. The two are virtually the same and confusion has been made worse by the liberation of Asiatic Ring-necks in Africa, though it is difficult to understand why. It is a bird of delicate shades of green, with blue on the upper back and in the long, narrow tail. It gets its name from the collar of black and pink which spreads round from the black chin; this collar is missing in the female. The bill is bright red. In the more highly populated parts of Asia this bird has become quite at home in the towns, nesting in holes and crevices in buildings – in wilder surroundings it uses holes in trees. It has a very swift, direct flight, banding itself in large flocks and unfortunately doing a lot of damage to crops, especially since it has the habit of gnawing and damaging far more than it actually eats. Probably no species of parrot is trapped in greater numbers for sale as pets than the Ring-neck, and Indian bird-markets present a pitiful spectacle because many of the captives will so obviously not survive long enough even to be sold, let alone to endure an ill-fed life in a tiny cage.

Lovebirds are small African parrots which are often confused in name with Budgerigars, though the two are quite dissimilar in appearance. Lovebirds, of which there are more than half-a-dozen species, are small, heavily-bodied parrots which get their name from the tendency of a pair to sit closely huddled together. However, their name belies their nature, since they can be very spiteful indeed, a trait which is sometimes all-too-evident in captivity, when they have a reputation for nipping off other birds' toes and even for murder. They have the very unusual habit among parrots of building a nest in the hole in which they have chosen to lay their eggs, and even more remarkable is the fact that the grass and other materials are carried up to the hole stuffed among their rump feathers instead of in the bill.

Australia has many species of fairly small, long-tailed parrakeets which are usually divided into the 'broadtail' group and the 'grass parrakeets'. The familiar Budgerigar is one of the latter. Pennant's Parrakeet – also called the Crimson Rosella or Lowry – is, in adult plumage, one of the most striking of this group, having its general plumage bright crimson, with violet cheeks and violet-blue wings with some very dark blue or black in them. The mantle is black, but the feathers have crimson edges. The central feathers of the tail are blue. This bird is about twice the size of a Budgerigar.

The 'Crow-pheasant', which is what the Common Coucal is frequently called in its native haunts, is neither a crow nor a pheasant but is really a cuckoo, though without the European Cuckoo's well-known habit of laying its eggs in other birds nests for foster parents to hatch and care for the young. However, visitors to India and the Far East had some excuse for their mistake because it spends most of its time on the ground, has a long tail, reddish-brown wings and pheasant-like flight and was no doubt frequently shot as a 'game-bird' by the uninitiated, which is probably the origin of its other name, Subaltern's Pheasant.

It is a native of India, Malaysia, Southern China and Indonesia and, although in poor light it may appear to be a rather dull brown and black bird, it springs to life in sunshine as a glossy purplish-blue bird with chestnut-red wings and a green sheen on its tail. It seems to like to be near water and is a bird of scrubby, rather open country with tall, coarse grass and bamboo clumps. It walks around on the ground searching for the small creatures on which it feeds.

Although so much a ground bird, its nest is rarely actually on the ground but may be anything from one to ten feet up in dense rank grasses or a bush. The foliage is bent over to form a domed structure with a fairly wide aperture at the side and seems much too small to accommodate the bird's long tail. It has a booming call or song, rather like a hollow repetition of the word 'boot', which is often uttered from the top of a bush on which it has been resting in the sun. Like other birds with 'booming' calls, it bends its bill downwards and seems to blow out its throat, appearing to put a great deal of effort into the performance.

*Above* The **White-breasted Kingfisher** (also known as the White-throated and White-fronted) is most unusually coloured in chocolate, blue, red and white and is one of the loveliest of a very beautiful family. Although it is classed among the 'forest' kingfishers it is often to be seen fishing, and this photograph was taken beside a stream in India.

*Right* Motmots, of which there are eight species, come from Central and South America and **Swainson's Motmot** is the only one which is found on the islands of Trinidad and Tobago. These birds are easily recognised by their long tails which have the two central feathers elongated and with a part of the shaft bare, leaving a 'racquet-shaped' tip. Another feature which is characteristic is their habit of swinging the tail sharply from side to side like a rather stiff pendulum, often leaving it stuck out sideways at one end of its swing for a considerable time.

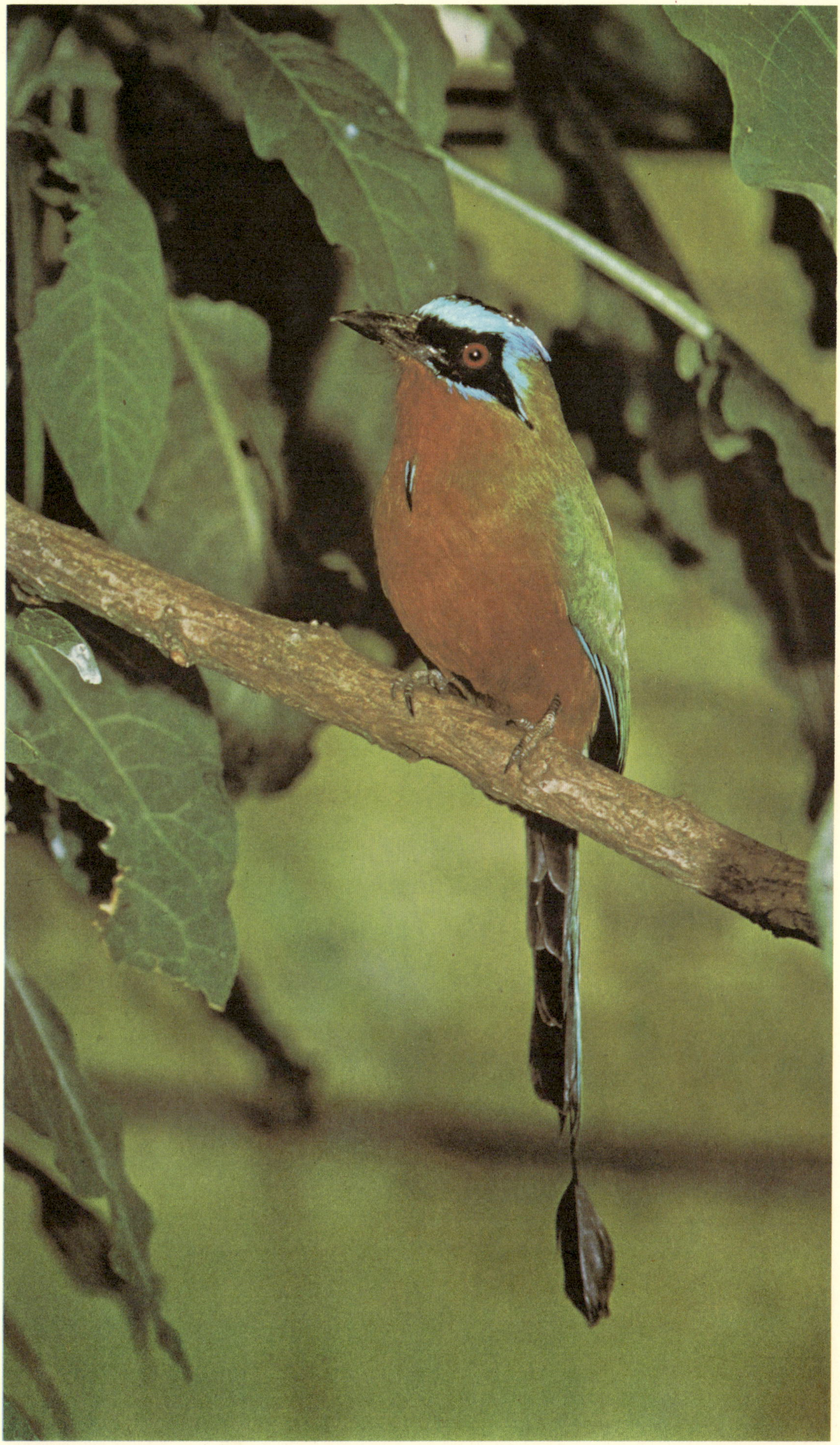

# Swifts and Hummingbirds

It may seem peculiar to place swifts and hummingbirds together in one chapter, since they appear to have little in common; to many people swifts are not unlike swallows, although they have in fact only a very superficial resemblance and are not closely related, while hummingbirds are frequently compared with insects. However, most modern systematists place both together in one 'order', the Apodiformes, and few people would question the fact that they both, in their different fashions, are masters of the air.

Some species of swifts and hummingbirds have something else in common: they have adapted their way of life to differing conditions of temperature and food supply by means which go far beyond those adopted by most other birds. For example, the Common Swift and the White-throated Swift have difficulty in finding sufficient food on the cold, wet or windy days which occur in some of the places in which they live, and if these conditions persist to starvation point the birds will clump together in crevices or holes in a semi-torpid condition, like animals which are hibernating. Matters become especially serious during the nesting period, but the eggs can be left for quite long periods, having a remarkable resistance to the effects of chilling, while the young birds can withstand several days of complete starvation by living on their reserves of fat or even by becoming torpid.

In a rather similar way, some hummingbirds become torpid at night, not necessarily as a result of cold but because in such small birds there is a great saving in calorie consumption during a state of torpidity as compared with ordinary sleep. It is interesting that a brooding female on a nest does not become torpid at night but retains its normal temperature, thus also maintaining the eggs or young at a normal temperature.

Swifts are mainly grey or brown birds with narrow, pointed wings and streamlined bodies. They are well named because they are among the fastest creatures which fly. Their flight is usually more direct and faster than that of martins and swallows and they tend to fly high with rapid wingbeats alternating with glides. Their wings often appear to be beating alternately and photography has shown that the beats do not always synchronize, thus aiding steering. They have small beaks but wide gapes for catching flying insects.

Swifts are the most aerial of all birds, catching their insect food entirely in the air, often spending the whole night 'roosting' in the air, and mating in the air. Since they find difficulty in rising from the ground, many swifts even take their nest material from the air, either catching odd scraps which have become airborne or snatching dried grasses and bits of vegetation as they fly low over them. Drinking and bathing is done in flight as they dip momentarily to the surface of the water. They have short ineffective-looking legs but strong claws, and when roosting, as many do, in caves or on cliffs and buildings, they cling to a vertical surface rather than sit across a perch.

They nest in a variety of places, from hollow trees, caves and crevices in cliffs (and of course buildings) to burrows in sand. Most of them glue the nest material together with saliva, but one species, the Palm Swift, actually glues its eggs to the side of a palm leaf, the bird hanging vertically to incubate them. Some species take over nests built by other birds, especially swallows.

The crested swifts are a family which inhabit India, Malaysia and eastwards from there to the Solomon Islands. They are unlike most other swifts in perching quite frequently and in building small cup-shaped nests which are just large enough to hold the single egg which is all that is laid. These nests are stuck to the side of a branch of a tree, and are too fragile to support the weight of the incubating bird, which clings to the branch instead.

Some species of swift (more properly called cave swiftlets) build their nests mainly or even entirely with their own salivary secretion, and these 'edible' nests are collected from India to the Philippines for making the famous birds' nest soup. Fortunately this trade – of which Borneo is the headquarters – is tending to decrease because young men no longer undertake so willingly the dangerous task of climbing in dark caves to find the nests.

It might be thought that such tiny and apparently frail birds as hummingbirds, with their high metabolic rate and diet consisting almost entirely of the nectar and nutrient insects from flowers, would be exclusively tropical. This is far from the case: over 300 species are found from Alaska in the north to the southern-most tip of South America. They are, however, far more numerous in the tropical countries than elsewhere and they are confined to the New World. The smallest members of the family – indeed the smallest known birds – are the bee hummingbirds of the West Indies. A Cuban species weighs less than two grams and is only the size of a large bumble-bee. At the other end of the scale is the Giant Hummingbird of the Andes, nearly nine inches from bill to tail, and one of the very few species whose wings flap slowly enough to be visible to human eyes.

The name hummingbird or 'hummer' comes from the noise made by the wings during flight. This flight is quite remarkable, since the birds are not only able to attain very high speeds in a forward direction but can hover motionless in the air, and they are the only birds which are known to be able to fly backwards. Most of their food is gathered while hovering in front of flowers, though they catch a certain amount of insect food on the wing. They are great bathers and some species cannot stay long in health without frequent wetting in rain, spray or the water trapped on large leaves.

Although some hummingbirds are rather drab in appearance, their name has come to be associated with brilliant colours and with a wonderful metallic lustre. Some have extraordinary plumes and crests or long trailing feathers in the tail. Perhaps the most remarkable thing of all about hummingbirds is the fact that the Ruby-throat, which breeds in North America and winters in tropical South America, on its twice-yearly migration flies non-stop the 500 or more miles over the waters of the Gulf of Mexico.

In most species, though not all, the female undertakes all the duties of nest-building, incubation and rearing of the young, since the male tends to desert his mate after courtship, which often includes the most amazingly intricate dances in the air. She builds a tiny cup-shaped nest – in the smaller species the nest is quite minute – of plant-down, tiny bits of vegetation and spiders' webs, balancing it on a branch or in a small fork, or among palm leaves, and she usually lays two white eggs. The young are born blind and nearly naked, but develop rapidly and can fly when they leave the nest at about three weeks old.

**Roller**. This beautiful bird is a good example of a species which breeds in south and east Europe but migrates to spend the winter in the tropics. At certain times of the year they are so numerous in parts of Tsavo National Park, Kenya, that it seems as though every other bush has one perched on its summit. It should not be confused with two rather similar species, the Abyssinian and Racquet-tailed Rollers, both of which however have tail feathers extended as long streamers.

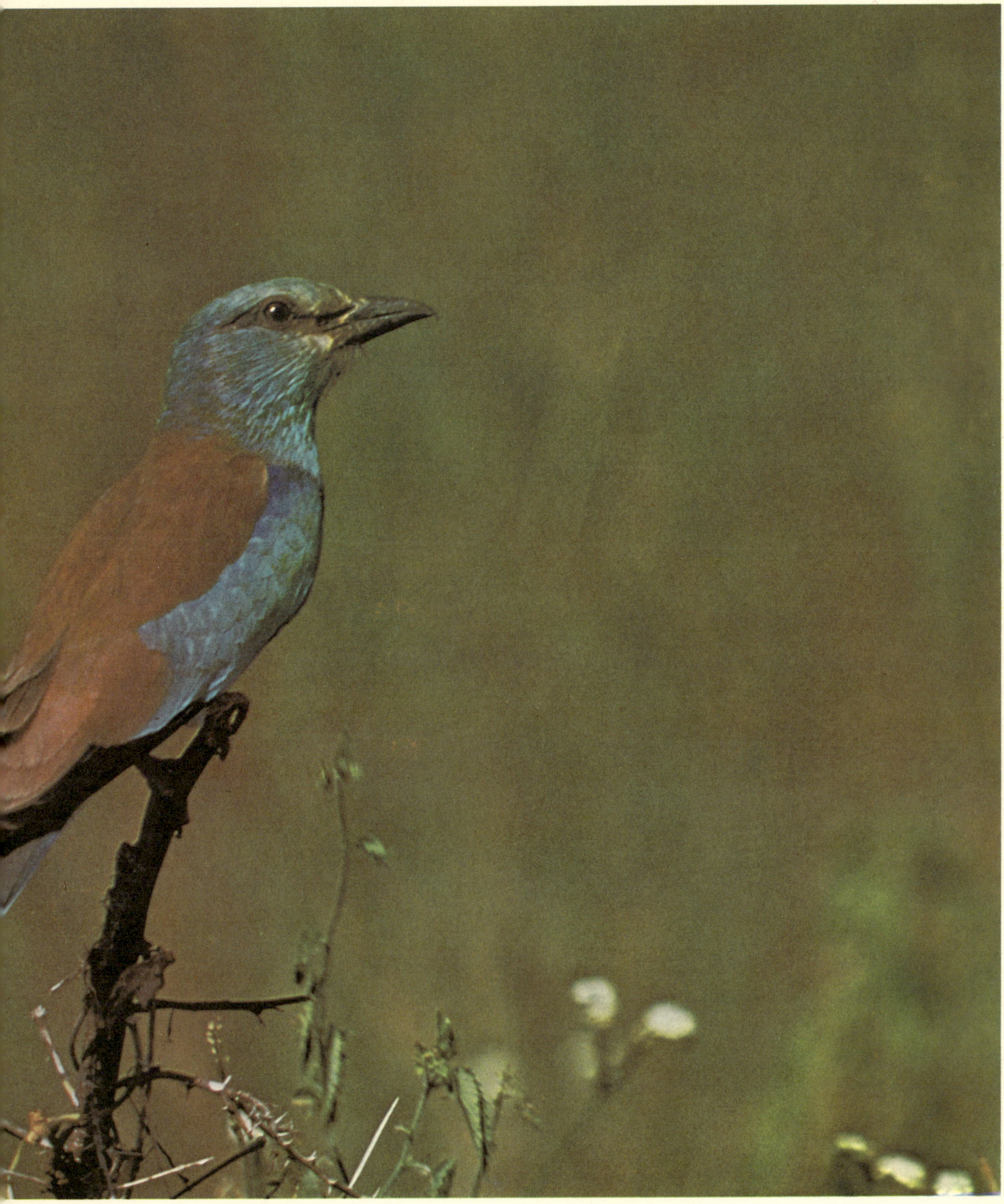

# From Kingfishers to Barbets

Kingfishers are rather dumpy, thick-set birds with long bills and short tails; most species have small inadequate-looking feet. The very word 'kingfisher' conjures up in most minds a bird of brilliant colours but, although true of most, not all kingfishers are colourful and some of the best known, for example the American Belted Kingfisher, the Pied Kingfishers of Africa and Asia and the Kookaburra or Laughing Kingfisher of Australia, are quite soberly clad. It may surprise many people to learn that by no means all kingfishers are catchers of fish or dwellers by water: some live deep in the forest, others in quite arid places, and their diet ranges from small insects to mice, rats and snakes.

The Pied Kingfisher (or Lesser Pied as it should be called, because of a larger and less known forest cousin) is one of the waterside ones. Its range extends across tropical Africa (except Somaliland), India, Burma, and into Malaysia. It is a common sight on East African rivers and lakes and may be seen on quite small jheels in India. It is larger than the familiar European Kingfisher – almost twice the size – and as its name implies, it is a study in black and white. Although it may perch on a branch overlooking the water to watch for fish beneath, it will also sit on mud banks almost at water level. It does not in fact need a vantage point at all, since it is expert at hovering over the water and finds much of its prey in this way. It nests in the typical kingfisher fashion, boring a tunnel in a river bank or sand pit. At the end is an enlarged chamber, the nest cavity in which the white eggs are laid.

While watching the rather soberly clad Lesser Pied Kingfisher in India, one may be startled to see, perhaps even on the same perch, one of the most beautiful of all members of the family, the White-breasted Kingfisher. This has an overall body colour of a very unusual chocolate-brown, with a quite dazzling blue back and wing edges, and a vivid white breast, and, to cap all, a coral-red bill. (This is replaced by a duller bill in the more south-easterly parts of the bird's range.) The bill is all the more startling because of its size; it seems at first disproportionately large for the bird, though not when it is seen in action with a fish which appears much too large for the bird to swallow. Although this is one of the 'fishing' kingfishers, it may commonly be spotted a long way from water, catching locusts and other large insects. At estuaries and sea-shores it can be seen to be very fond of small crabs.

Unlike the shrill whistle of the Common Kingfisher, the call of the White-breasted Kingfisher is a loud, screaming, argumentative cackle, broadcast from a perch or in flight during the nuptial display. The bird's nesting habits are, however, typical, a hole with a nesting chamber at the far end being bored into a river bank or small cliff which is sometimes of a surprisingly hard composition.

The Malachite Kingfisher is found over most of tropical Africa, its range extending right down to the Cape. It is one of the smallest members of the family and superficially it has a resemblance to the Common Kingfisher: it has a royal blue back, wings and tail, red cheeks, throat and underparts, white patches at the sides of the nape and a large brilliant red bill. Its most obvious difference lies in the crown of the head, which is of a different blue from the rest of the body: it is malachite blue (some people might call it green) with black and white markings. These crown feathers are erectile and can be raised when the bird is excited or alarmed, but instead of becoming a neat crest the feathers then look unkempt, as though the bird needed a thorough preening.

The Malachite Kingfisher is almost entirely a water-feeder, diving after small fish and other aquatic creatures. Time after time it returns to the same perch, where it sits silently and still, apart from an occasional bobbing of the head to judge the distance of a possible tit-bit – until it plunges headfirst into the water again.

Where suitable sand or earth banks are available it will use them for its nest hole, but in their absence it will bore into a termite mound, which it may share with bee-eaters and a mongoose family and, sometimes, the termites, since it does not necessarily choose a deserted mound. In the chamber at the end of its tunnel it lays three to five eggs on the bare earth or sand, building no nest for them. However, a 'nest' of regurgitated fish bones and other matter accumulates when the young have hatched and it is noticeable that the Malachite, like many other kingfishers, dives into the water for a quick bath after leaving what must soon become a very messy nest.

The young are fed on fish and other small water creatures of gradually increasing size and it is interesting that one can tell whether a kingfisher is going to eat its prey itself or pass it to its mate or young. If it is the former, the fish's head will be turned to face down the catcher's throat; if intended for delivery to another bird, the head of the fish will point outwards. This is because fish simply *must* be swallowed headfirst to avoid damage to the throat of the eater by the sharp spines on the fins of the fish.

Near to the kingfishers in scientific order are the colourful bee-eaters which are predominantly tropical and are found only in the Old World. There are twenty-four species and, although their colours vary greatly, they are alike in their streamlined shape and way of life. They catch their insect food in the air during the most graceful flight, sometimes dashing out from a perch like a fly-catcher and returning to it repeatedly. They live socially, sometimes in huge colonies.

The chief colour in most species is blue or green, while red and yellow and white are found in many. As their name suggests, their principal food is bees or wasps, but even large dragon-flies are swallowed whole. They gather round bush fires to catch the fleeing insects and follow locust swarms, doing good to everybody except bee-keepers, by whom they are naturally disliked.

It has often been suggested that some species of bee-eater catch fish from the surface of the water. This has yet to be proved, and it seems more likely that they are engaged in drinking or bathing. It is not difficult to watch the only European member of the family doing this, and the bird can quite clearly be seen not only to catch nothing but to repair to a perch after several plunges, there to have a very thorough preen.

Like kingfishers, bee-eaters bore nest holes in banks or termites' nests, sometimes in such numbers that an area of sand bank will be so riddled with holes as to look like a vast Sand Martin colony. Both sexes share in the domestic duties and it is an amusing sight to watch a bird burrowing, head inwards, scrabbling so fast with its tiny feet that a shower of sand flies out under its tail.

A good tropical example of the family is the White-throated, sometimes called the Black-crowned, Bee-eater of Africa and the south-west corner of Arabia. Although not one of the most brightly coloured members of the family, it has a delicate beauty which is enhanced by the extremely long and thin central tail feathers, which project four inches or more beyond the rest of the tail. The upperparts are pale green shading into a beautiful blue on the rump; the crown of the head is black and between this and the green back the nape is golden-yellow; a white forehead continues round over the eyes as a narrow band, while a broad black band passes through and below the eye. The throat is white with a broad black border beneath; below this again is a narrow, pale blue band shading into the very pale greenish-blue of the breast; this in turn shades into white on the belly. The wings are green, flecked with blue and becoming predominantly blue towards the tail, but when in flight glimpses of yellow, and even pale orange-red, appear unexpectedly in the wings.

The **Tree Pie**, an inhabitant of India and Burma, although not gaudy is pleasingly and rather unusually coloured. It is a woodland bird which does not hesitate to enter gardens and it will eat practically anything from kitchen scraps and fruit to the tiny young of other species. Unlike the European Magpie it builds an open nest with no roof, usually in a fork well up in a tree.

The White-throated Bee-eater's way of life is generally similar to its relatives, but it has a habit of making its sorties after food from low perches and sometimes from the ground. It also takes food from the ground, where it looks rather out of place as it hops around picking up insects and small lizards.

Although it is only a short step from bee-eaters to rollers, and the latter are as brightly coloured as the former, rollers have none of the slim and streamlined appearance of bee-eaters, being rather thick-set crow-like birds with large heads and stout bills and broad, rounded wings. However, a roller in flight – especially in its tumbling rolling nuptial flight from which it gets its name – is quite breathtaking in its beauty, and stout and clumsy though they may appear when hopping on the ground or clinging to the entrance of their nest hole, once airborne they show how strong on the wing they are and how acrobatic is their flight when displaying or evading a passing predator. Since many species have the most brilliant blues in their wing-feathers, they show themselves, not only as masters of aerial control, but as being among the most beautifully coloured of all birds.

Most rollers (there are about a dozen species) are birds of tropical lands. They are found in most parts of Africa, and through India, Malaysia and Indonesia to New Guinea and northern Australia. However there is one species, the European Roller, which spends only the winters in the tropics, migrating to breed well north of the tropical zone. Another species, the Broadbilled (or Broad-mouthed) Dollar Bird, although having a very wide tropical distribution from India to the Solomon Islands, spreads out of the tropics into Manchuria and Japan. This bird should not be confused with the African Broad-billed Roller, which is a quite different species.

The Indian Roller, or Blue Jay as it is sometimes mis-called, appears at rest as a rusty-red bird with a blue crown and tail, while in flight it is miraculously changed into a gorgeous blue bird with a little red on it. In fact the nape, back and cheeks are a rusty-red, shading on the breast into paler red splashed with blue and into pale blue on the belly and under-tail. The wings are a mixture of Oxford and Cambridge blues and the tail is also blue. It is a bird of open country with scattered trees, choosing an elevated perch from which it watches for a locust or other small creature to move on the ground below. Like other members of its family it breeds in holes in trees and rocks, sometimes choosing a crevice in the masonry of an old building. It makes little or no nest but lays its eggs on the rubbish which has collected on the floor of the cavity. The young are fed on a variety of small animals, from cockchafers to lizards.

The European Roller is a good example of a medium-sized bird which breeds in a temperate climate but migrates south to spend the winter in the tropics. Indeed, so numerous are they in some parts of East Africa, in the early part of the year, that it seems as though there is a roller sitting on the top of every bush. This becomes more nearly true when a relative, the Lilac-breasted Roller, is taken into account. These also watch and wait on the tops of stumps and bushes and some may be seen in tropical Africa at the same time as the more numerous European Roller. However, they are by no means all merely visitors for the winter: some are resident and spend the whole year in East Africa. Others have come south from their breeding area in Ethiopia and Somalia, while others again are visitors from South Africa. A good many of them are nomadic out of their breeding season, moving because of weather or food supply.

Only one thing tends to spoil the otherwise unexcelled beauty of the Lilac-breasted Roller – the fact that 'its hair always looks untidy'. It is curious that the feathers on the crown of its head are rarely neatly compressed but tend to look fluffed-up in the wind. Despite this it is generally considered to be the most beautiful member of an outstandingly attractive family and it has been claimed to be Africa's most lovely bird. Those thousands of visitors to one of Kenya's most famous nature reserves, Tsavo National Park, most of whom have almost certainly gone there to see elephants, must be blind indeed if they fail to see and appreciate the beauty of the innumerable rollers of these two species with which they are literally surrounded.

Another short step, although not such an obvious one, brings us from rollers to Hoopoes; but the Hoopoe, which looks so very much a tropical bird (perhaps exotic is a better word) is not confined to the tropics. In summer it breeds as far north as Moscow, and a few reach Britain each year. It also occurs down through South Africa to the Cape. The Hoopoe is another hole-nester, the holes being in trees, buildings or even underground. It is also

*Right* Unlike its cousin illustrated on page 60–1, the **Lilac-breasted Roller** is resident in Africa, although those from north-east Africa tend to move south out of the breeding season. If possible this bird is even more beautiful than the European Roller but its feathers, especially on the head, tend in the slightest breeze to become ruffled, giving it all too frequently a rather untidy look. It should be looked for on telegraph wires and the tops of bushes, whence it floats down on to a grasshopper or beetle.

*Below* While it is not the most brilliantly coloured member of its family, the **White-throated Bee-eater** has two claims to distinction: it has extremely long and thin central tail feathers which project at least four inches beyond the tail proper, and it is more likely than its relations to be seen on the ground, from which it picks up some of its food and where it may sometimes be seen running about after beetles and other small creatures.

Hornbills are birds of the Old World tropics and the forty-five species range from Africa across Asia as far as the Solomon Islands. This **Red-billed Hornbill**, photographed in Africa, is one of the smaller species and is the one most likely to be noticed by the casual visitor because, instead of being rather wary as most species are, it has learnt in some places that man is not always dangerous but may be a source of food. The author once had the experience of a male Red-billed Hornbill returning to him time after time for pieces of sardine sandwich to take to the female and chicks sealed up in their nest-hole.

vividly coloured but does not compete with the blues and greens of bee-eaters and rollers: its body colour is rusty- or sandy-pink, with the lower back, wings and tail providing a startling contrast with their bands of black and white. Even more arresting is the Hoopoe's crest: it is a sandy colour with black bars, forming at rest an extension to the back of the head which, with the long, curved bill, resembles nothing so much as a rather bizarre pick-axe. However, at the slightest excitement or alarm, or when something arouses curiosity, the crest is erected fan-wise like a cockatoo's, with a bowing of the head, showing the black and white bars at the tips of the feathers. It is an interesting point that this crest is always erected as the bird alights after flying, whether on a perch or on the ground.

Beautiful (or bizarre, whichever way you look at it) as the Hoopoe is, it has a most unattractive characteristic: the young in the nest hole, and the brooding female, produce from their oil-glands a secretion with a most revolting smell. When this is added to the fact that little if any nest sanitation is carried out, the state of the nest by the time the young are three weeks old can be better imagined than described.

Hoopoes feed on a wide variety of small animals, for which they probe and search rather than wait and watch. Their long thin bill goes far into crevices and can be driven deep into the ground; they have also been known to 'drum' with it on dead wood to dislodge insects. Grasshoppers and mole-crickets are favourite items, but lizards and scorpions are commonly taken.

Hornbills are birds of the Old World tropics and are widely distributed from West Africa through Asia as far as the Solomon Islands but, although they come very near, they do not occur in Australia. They are so named because of their enormous bill, sometimes surmounted by a large casque, which gives them a top-heavy appearance although they are good fliers, alternating a few strong flaps with long glides with outspread wings. The huge bill, which looks so heavy, is in reality quite light because it is not solid but contains a honeycomb of cellular bony tissue. One exception to this is the large Helmeted Hornbill, from Malaya and Borneo, whose bill is of solid ivory It is carved into many kinds of ornaments, especially by the Chinese who prize it greatly as an adornment which is only allowed to be worn by high-ranking people.

No hornbill can be described as beautiful, but they are fascinating – if rather grotesque – birds with some remarkable and most interesting habits. Most species have comparatively small slender bodies and long tails and thin necks which accentuate the large size of the bill. They are mainly inhabitants of at least partially wooded country, from the savanna of Africa with its patches of open acacia woods, to dense tropical rain forest. The African ground hornbills differ not only in their habitat, which is open rough grassland, but in having longer legs and a stockier body which, especially since they spend nearly all their time on the ground, gives them the appearance of a large-headed turkey, which they also resemble in size.

The forty-five species of hornbill eat both fruit and small creatures of many kinds, though the species differ in their particular choice, some apparently being almost exclusively insectivorous. The large ground hornbills will eat almost anything and have been recorded as banding together to tackle snakes.

By far the most remarkable thing about the hornbills is their method of nesting and rearing their young. They lay their eggs – from one in the largest species to five or six in the smaller ones – in holes in trees, the aperture being reduced to a mere slit just large enough to admit the tip of the bill by 'plastering-up' with mud or dung mixed with saliva. This is done chiefly by the female from inside the hole with mud brought in small lumps by her mate, so that she walls herself in for the whole period of incubation and at least a part of the time when the young are being reared. While she is thus immured she goes through a very rapid and extensive moult. She avoids the nest becoming too fouled by turning round and forcefully defaecating through the slit, as also do the youngsters after a certain age. She and the chicks are of course entirely dependent on the male for food during this time, and when she does finally break out the young re-plaster the hole with a mixture of their own droppings, food remains and saliva. The two parents continue to feed the young for a considerable further period until they in their turn start pecking away at the rock-hard barrier to free themselves. The females of some of the large fruit-eating hornbills stay with their offspring (often only one or two) until they are ready to fly, and then all break out together. Females of various species have been recorded as staying walled-in for over one hundred days, and even such comparatively small birds as Red-billed Hornbills are commonly sealed up for over seventy days. The only exception to this most interesting procedure is in the case of the two species of ground hornbill which, although they nest in holes in trees like other species, have never been recorded as mudding-up the entrance.

Hornbills are often confused with toucans, which also have enormous bills: indeed toucans' bills are even larger than those of hornbills, although they lack the remarkable casques of the latter. They make up for this in most cases by having their bills brilliantly coloured, and their bodies are more strikingly clad, almost every colour being represented among the thirty-seven species. Despite this they are surprisingly difficult to see in the trees where they live.

Toucans are confined to the American tropics, and they were named 'tucans' by the Indians of Brazil. Despite their similarity to hornbills they are not closely related to them and have not the same nesting habits. They nest in tree holes, but do not wall-in the female and youngsters: on the contrary, in some species a number of adults will crowd into the nest hole at night to roost alongside the chicks and may even take turns at feeding them during the day.

Toucans are mainly fruit-eaters, taking in addition small creatures such as insects and the tiny young of other birds. They enjoy each other's company, going through antics which look remarkably like play, leaping over each other, seizing each other's bills and performing mutual preening. They lay from two to four white eggs and the young are hatched completely naked and with their eyes closed. They are very slow to develop and remain in the nest for at least six weeks. Adults adopt a most peculiar position while roosting so that they look more like fluffy balls than birds: they lay their long bill down the centre of their back, then fold the tail forward to cover it.

Barbets are thick-set birds with short necks and stout, sometimes long, bills and are typical tropical-forest birds of America, Asia and Africa. The seventy-two species vary from tiny birds only three and a half inches long to those of pigeon size, about twelve inches long. They nest in holes and, although they will occasionally take over an existing natural hole or disused one of another species they usually bore their own, after the fashion of woodpeckers or kingfishers, into rotten trees or sand banks. Sometimes termites' nests are burrowed into and D'Arnaud's Barbet in Africa drills more or less perpendicularly downward into the ground. It is remarkable how small a nest cavity can be used if the tree in which it is made has no room for anything larger. Gaudy Barbets from Malaysia, which are eight and a half inches long, have been recorded as using cavities in trees the trunk of which is only five inches in diameter. It is astounding to see a bird wriggle head-first down a hole barely large enough to accommodate it, only to re-appear a few moments later again head-uppermost. How it found room to turn at the bottom is a mystery, and during incubation the birds must have sat virtually folded up, with bill and tail pointing upwards. Barbets' eggs are white and the parents share all the domestic duties. The young remain in the nest longer than many birds of their size and are well developed when they emerge.

Barbets are mainly fruit-eaters, though most species relish an occasional insect, while a few live chiefly if not entirely on small insects. When taking fruit they are very wasteful feeders, plucking and rejecting many of the berries and small fruits which they attack, while they so persistently shake their heads to rid themselves of pieces of fruit which stick to them that more seems to be cast away than is swallowed. Some of the insect-feeding species cling to trees like woodpeckers, working their way over the bark and hammering into rotten wood in their search for food and, although they do not have such stiff tail feathers as the woodpeckers have developed for the purpose, they not infrequently support themselves on their tail as they hang upright against the tree.

Barbets have a wide variety of colours, from drab greys and browns to brilliant reds, blues and yellows, on a generally bright green body. Indeed, as mentioned above, one of the Malaysian species is aptly named the Gaudy Barbet, although even this is perhaps not the most brightly coloured of all: certainly some of the South American species are very beautiful indeed.

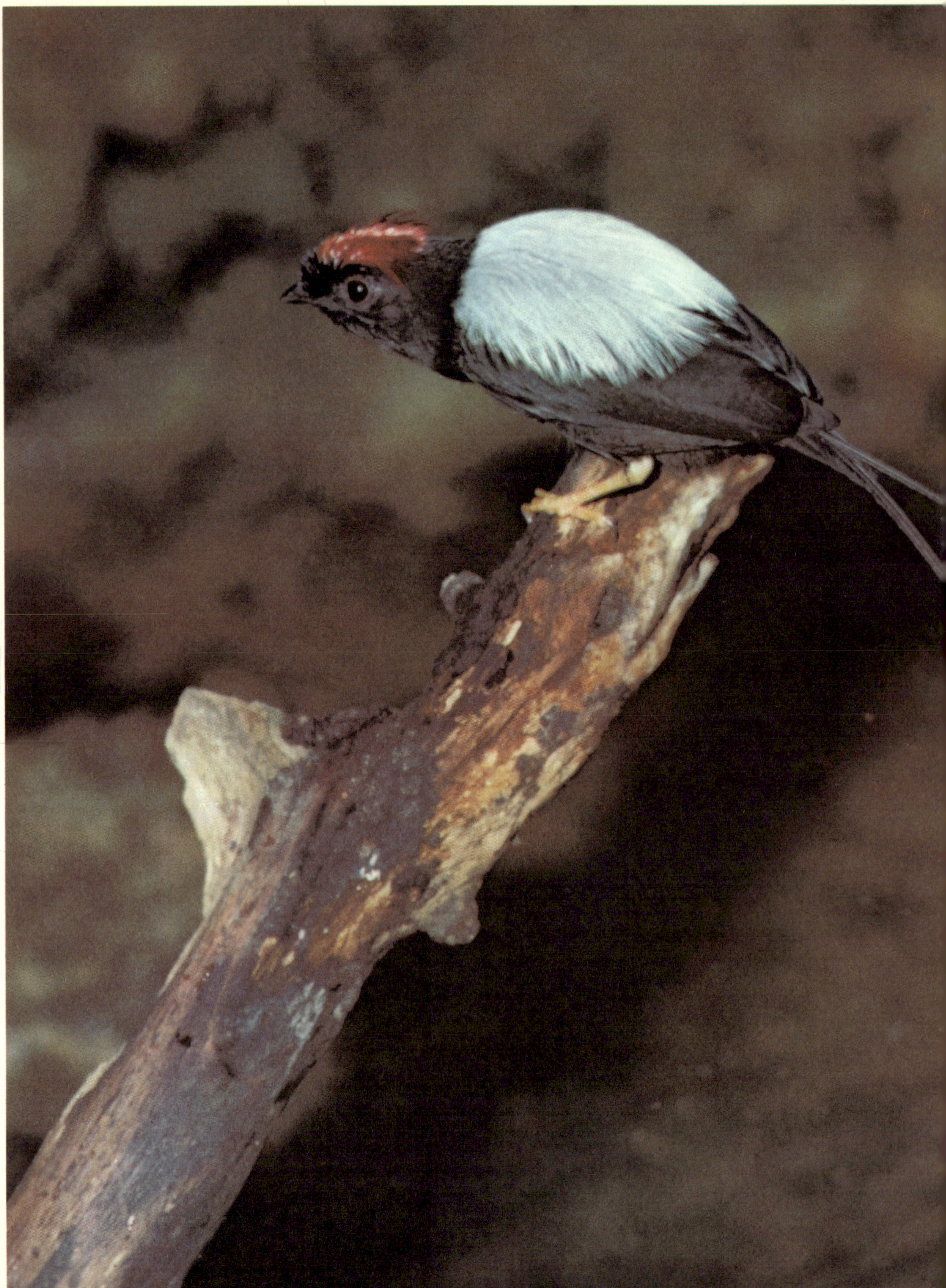

*Left* Manakins, of which the **Long-tailed Manakin** is a beautiful example, are little birds which are restricted to tropical Central and South America, including some of the islands. They indulge in the most remarkable nuptial dances, varying with the different species, although after mating the males take no further part in the raising of a family. Although formerly the name was pronounced in the same way as that of the mannikins — to which they are quite unrelated — there is a growing feeling that confusion could be avoided if they were called, or at least pronounced, 'manarkins'.

*Above* Most pittas are strikingly coloured and this **Banded Pitta** is no exception. They are ground dwellers and inhabit the darker parts of the forests. Various species are found over most of the tropical parts of the Old World, but especially in south-east Asia and Malaysia, the tropical species being joined in winter by others from further north. Pittas feed on small living creatures, mainly insects; some are especially fond of termites.

# Perching Birds

Over 5,000 species of birds – that is over half the known species – are lumped together in a vast order known as the Passeriformes, or perching birds. It includes the true song birds and the members range in size from the ravens down to the tiniest wrens, kinglets and waxbills. All the families in the order consist of land birds, which are world-wide in their distribution except at the poles.

The feet of all perching birds are similar in structure: all have four toes which are free and mobile and are joined at the same level, with the hallux (the equivalent of the 'big toe' of many other animals) highly developed and pointing backwards so that it opposes the other toes to give a firm grip. The foot is thus well adapted to perching and in fact has developed the muscles and tendons in such a way that the toes grip all the tighter if the bird tends to fall backwards from its perch. The toes of passerine birds are never webbed, even in those few members of the order which have become adapted to a semi-aquatic way of life.

The list of perching birds is usually headed by the broadbills, a family of large-eyed, broad-headed, rather plump birds from the tropics of the Old World, ranging from Africa to the Philippines. Their name is derived from the wide gape of the bill when fully opened. The Asiatic broadbills are mainly colourful birds – three species are bright green and one is red, black and white with a blue bill; the African ones are generally rather duller and are clad in browns and greys relieved with red or white. The fourteen species range from five to eleven inches long.

All broadbills are expert nest builders. Although the nests vary somewhat in design according to the species, they are all pear-shaped structures which are suspended from a branch – often over water – by a quite slender woven string of fibres and grasses, the main nest being entered from the side by a hole which often has an overhanging porch. In some species more than the pair which actually own the nest will take part in its construction, and in some cases as many as ten birds have been watched hard at work on one nest.

The best known of the cotingas, a very varied family from the tropical parts of America, are the two species of Cock-of-the-rock, birds which scarcely need description. The male of one species is red and that of the other orange-yellow. Both have a remarkable helmet of feathers almost completely hiding the bill. These birds live mainly on or near the ground in deep forests and our knowledge of their habits is very incomplete. The few nests which have been found have been made largely of mud and small pieces of vegetable matter, stuck on a small ledge or a rock face near a jungle stream. The birds have a courtship display in which up to twenty of them gather to dance in a forest clearing.

It is rather surprising that the quite large Cock-of-the-rock is closely related to the tiny tit-like manakins, which also come from tropical America, and which should not be confused with the mannikins, small finch-like seed-eating birds from the Old World tropics. Manakins also have an elaborate courtship, which varies from one species to another, but in some consists of a dance performed by the male in a small clearing made by himself deep in the forest, in which he goes through remarkable hops and jumps and little flights, accompanied by curious popping and buzzing noises made by the wings. The females visit the males in their little courts and in some species join in the dances with them. The nest is like a miniature hammock in the fork of a small shrub, often near or even over water. Two eggs are laid by most manakins and it is one of the comparatively few small passerine birds in which, so far as is known, the male after mating takes no part in raising the family.

Pittas are small, plump, upstanding birds with scarcely any tail, and they are about the size of a thrush. Most of the twenty-three species are gaudily coloured, the females of most looking similar to the males except that their plumage may be slightly duller. However, in a few species the plumage of the sexes is strikingly different. They range across the Old World tropics from Africa across Asia to Australia.

Pittas make rather rough oval nests of leaves and various kinds of vegetable matter, like a loosely-knit football with a hole low in one side. They are built low down in the forest, either on the ground, on a broken stump or in among broken sticks.

No book on birds, tropical or otherwise, would be complete without some mention of the crows, even if only because they are considered by many authorities to be the most highly-developed family of birds and to represent the furthest stage in evolution. Included in the crow family are magpies, jays, choughs, ravens and a number of birds with distinctive names. Although the word 'crow' conjures up a picture of a bird which is entirely black, some members of the family are very brightly and beautifully coloured, blues and browns being quite usual, while the Hunting Cissa or Green Magpie of tropical Asia is apple-green with a bright red bill.

Most crows are bold and rather aggressive birds, tending in many species to live and breed in large communities. Although a few species are specialists in their feeding, many members of the family are virtually omnivorous, eating anything from carrion to fruit and even quite small insects, while small animals of all sorts are relished and other birds' eggs and young are especially vulnerable to nearly all crows. They hold down an item of food in one foot in order to pluck pieces from it with the bill.

Birds of paradise are relatives of the crows and New Guinea and adjacent places are the areas in which most species are found. They are mostly rather large birds, about pigeon size, living in forest trees, often at great altitudes in mountain forests. They eat a great deal of fruit but will take insects and small lizards and frogs. Most species live a solitary life except at breeding time, although a number may sometimes be seen together when attracted to a tree covered in ripe fruit.

Birds of paradise vary greatly in that in some species the sexes are more or less alike in plumage whereas in others there is a great difference, the males being brightly coloured or adorned with striking plumes (sometimes both) while the females are very dull, ordinary-looking birds. It is interesting that those species in which the sexes are alike form pairs, the male assisting in raising the family, while those with great sexual differences are polygamous, the female alone being responsible for nesting duties. The males of this latter type indulge in fantastic displays, either on the ground in clearings which they have made or high in the trees, in which case a number of males may gather in a communal display. These displays make use of the plumes and other ornamentations of the males, which go through remarkable dances and posturings, in some cases even hanging upside down from a branch.

The breeding habits are little known (for some species not at all) but most nests are loosely made and are rather large cup-shaped affairs, although the smallest and perhaps most brilliantly coloured member of the family, the King Bird of Paradise, uses holes in trees. Birds of paradise are among the few birds which are known to hybridize in the wild.

Nuthatches are compact, active, tree-climbing little birds with short tails, strong toes and claws and a woodpecker-like bill. All members of the family spend much of their time clinging rather than perching and one is a rock-dweller. They appear to run like mice up, down and along trees and even underneath horizontal branches, although in fact their progression is mainly by rapid hops. A number of species are found in the tropics. Three from southern Asia, the Velvet-fronted, Azure and Beautiful Nuthatches, are brightly coloured, unlike most members of the family which are mainly grey, brown and white. Nearly all species have a black eye-stripe.

**Ruppell's Robin Chat** and the very similar White-browed Robin Chat would be difficult to tell apart were it not for the former's black central tail feathers; both are inhabitants of tropical East Africa. Most robin chats have beautiful songs, mimicking the notes of other birds, and sometimes they have a curious ventriloquial effect making it difficult to tell where the song is coming from.

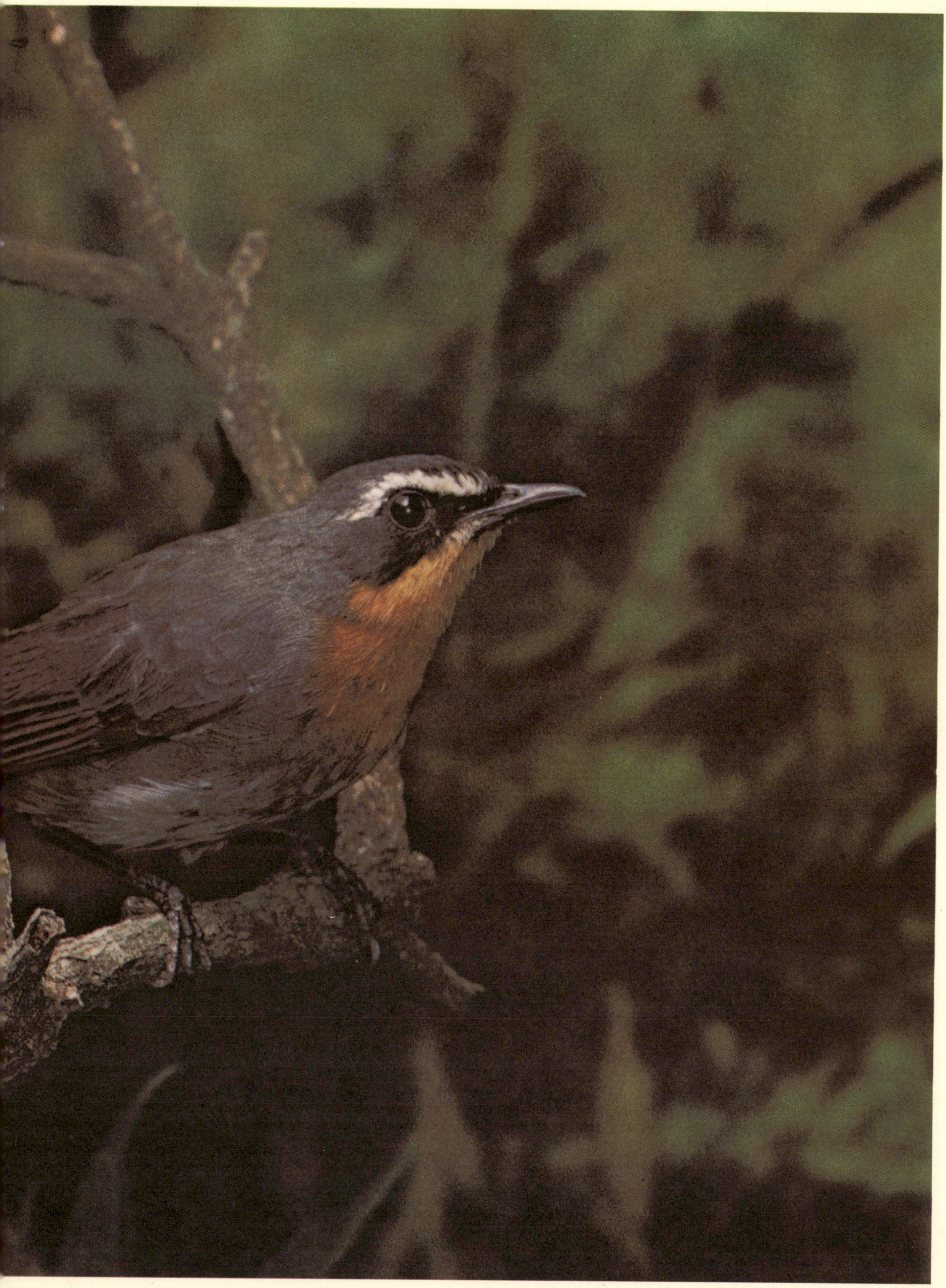

Although some species build open nests or use rock or tree crevices, many take over a natural hole in a tree – or one made by another bird – and plaster up the entrance hole until it is just a tight fit for themselves. One tropical species, the Chestnut-bellied Nuthatch of India, Burma and Thailand, in addition to reducing the size of the hole, builds a canopy of mud and roots inside the tree cavity. The display of the male of this species at nesting time is delightful: a bout of loud calling is succeeded by a gentle, seductive 'whit-whit-whit' rapidly repeated, as he lands on the upper surface of a large horizontal branch, beside the female but a little in front of her. Fluttering his wings and spreading his tail to expose the white marks, he writhes his extended head from side to side and round and round in a manner remarkably snake-like. At the same time he follows the retreating female, both birds moving sideways in a series of jerky hops, until she assumes a crouching position ready for mating.

Incubation of the eggs is performed by the female alone, but both parents share in feeding the young, chiefly on insects. If these are too large to be swallowed whole they are wedged in a crevice in the bark of a tree and small pieces broken off. Outside the breeding season many nuts and seeds are eaten.

The Rufous Bush-chat is a bird with a most interesting distribution. It occurs in two wide bands, one the whole width of northern tropical Africa, the other much further north, all along the Mediterranean coast of north Africa westwards to India, with northward 'extensions' to the southern part of the Iberian peninsula, Greece, Turkey and south-west Russia. The most remarkable thing about this distribution is that, while the tropical African birds are sedentary, those from the northern band of their range are migratory and their wintering-grounds coincide almost exactly with the tropical area in which the others spend the entire year.

Rufous Bush-chats are the size of a small thrush, with an alert stance, frequently cocking and fanning their tail to show the arresting black and white extremities of the tail feathers. They spend much of their time on the ground and make themselves conspicuous, unlike the Nightingale to which, apart from their tail, they are often likened. Those from the north-eastern part of the range scarcely deserve the name 'rufous', since they are a much duller brown. They prefer a dry, almost arid, habitat and are much given to taking dust baths and crouching on the ground with eyes closed as though they were taking a siesta. When prickly pears are present they are a favourite nesting-place.

Rather larger, though not dissimilar in their bold, thrush-like stance, are the robin-chats. They are found in the tropical parts of East Africa and, like many members of the large thrush family, have beautiful flute-like songs. Some – for example the White-browed Robin-chat and Ruppell's Robin-chat – are wonderful mimics and incorporate into their songs the notes of many other birds.

Bird-watching visitors to the tropics may well be confused by the large numbers of 'small brown jobs'. Some of the most widespread of these are the grass or fantail warblers of the genus *Cisticola*, of which there are no fewer than seventy-five species, some being very difficult indeed to separate in the field. East Africa alone has twenty-nine species. All are small, rather inconspicuous brown birds, streaked above and lighter-coloured below, and all build neat nests of various designs near the ground, making use of cobwebs and plant down to fashion beautiful little hanging purses, sometimes domed over.

The 'Common' Fantail Warbler has, like the Rufous Bush-chat, a most interesting distribution. In Asia it spreads right across India, Burma, south China, Thailand and the southern Indonesian islands to northern Australia. Apart from the heavily forested areas it occupies the whole of Africa south of the Sahara, and it has a curiously patchy distribution around the Mediterranean Sea. It is to be found in many types of habitat: reed-beds, marshy places, corn fields, roadsides and patches of waste land, dry savanna and in fact almost all types of open ground. A skulking secretive bird, it is difficult to see except during the breeding season, when the song of the male as he sings 'zip, zip, zip', high in the air, makes him conspicuous. As he flies and sings he describes a series of sharp undulations, with a 'zip' coinciding with each wave. Round and round he goes beating the bounds of his territory, apparently working very hard and flying quite a distance but, in reality, covering very little ground. The species is both sedentary and migratory, most birds straying only a little from their breeding grounds, although it is known that many of those breeding in eastern Asia move for the winter to warmer areas further south.

Three to seven eggs are laid in the well-hidden nest, five being the usual number. The young in the nest make a remarkably loud noise for such tiny birds. They are fed by both parents on insects and even when quite young, that is when very tiny indeed, they are given insects of a size which one would have thought it impossible for them to swallow. The male approaches the nest, beak full, still singing his monotonous though curiously charming song, and one of the ways to find the otherwise rather difficult-to-discover nest is to watch where he alights at the finish of one of his shorter song-flights.

Shrikes are bold and aggressive birds with hooked bills and sharp claws and more like birds of prey than any other passerine birds, although they are not large, being mainly about thrush-size or smaller. They eat small birds, mammals, lizards and many kinds of large insects, and fruit has been recorded. Some species have earned the name 'butcher-bird' from their habit of impaling prey on thorns; this not only aids them to tear the food apart but in at least some cases acts as a store or 'larder' to which they return when food is scarce or bad weather makes it difficult to hunt. Shrikes tend to sit on high exposed perches – often using telegraph wires – to watch for prey on the ground beneath, although many insects and birds are caught in flight. A few species hunt among the undergrowth and others again run around on the ground searching for food.

Although opinions differ, shrikes are usually divided into three sub-families, the true shrikes, the bush shrikes and the helmet shrikes; examples of all three are found in the tropics. A typical true shrike, and one of the most beautifully (though not gaudily) coloured is the Rufous-backed Shrike whose range extends from India south-east to New Guinea.

Most shrikes are solitary except when breeding, although the Bay-backed Shrike of India and some of the species of fiscal shrike of Africa spend much of their time in small parties.

Shrikes build rather loosely-made shallow-cupped nests in bushes and low trees, though many are neatly lined with fine hairs and roots; some birds add pieces of coloured paper and other unlikely objects which they find in their territory. Both sexes share in raising a brood – although usually the female alone incubates – and some members of the family are very bold in defence of their nest and young, swooping repeatedly at the head of an intruder.

Some of the bush shrikes, which are found only in Africa, are most gaudily coloured, two of them – the Four-coloured and Doherty's Bush Shrikes – being bright green on top, golden-yellow to orange beneath, with a crimson throat patch and black breast-band. The chief difference between these two is that the former has a greenish-yellow forehead and the latter a crimson one.

Starlings are medium-sized birds, usually lively and cheerfully garrulous, chattering to each other continually. Some species are wonderful mimics, the common Palaearctic Starling copying other birds' songs, for example the Curlew's bubbling call, so well as to mislead bird watchers, while the Hill Mynah has long been famous as a much better imitator of the human voice than any parrot.

Although starlings are primarily Old World birds and most species are tropical, they have unwisely been introduced by man into almost every corner of the world, South America alone having so far escaped.

Some of the tropical African starlings are among the most beautiful members of the family: some indeed may claim to be in the top rank of beauty of the birds of the world. The rather local Golden-breasted or Regal Starling from Ethiopia, Somaliland and south through eastern Kenya to the north-east of Tanzania, is perhaps the most beautiful of all. It is slim for a starling, with a long greenish tail, brilliant iridescent blue upperparts, green-blue head and throat and the most vivid golden-yellow belly. It is usually shy and unapproachable, and most visitors to East Africa count themselves lucky to have a distant and rather fleeting glimpse of this gorgeous bird. However, rather out of character a few pairs in Tsavo Park West, in Kenya, have overcome their fear of man and their usual love of termites as food to such an extent that they will take food thrown to them by visitors or even take it from the plates of diners at table.

If it were not so very much more common and widespread, the Superb Starling, also from East Africa, would be a close competitor in good looks. It differs in both looks and temperament. A typical dumpy 'starling-shaped' bird with a shortish tail, it has greenish-blue upperparts with a metallic

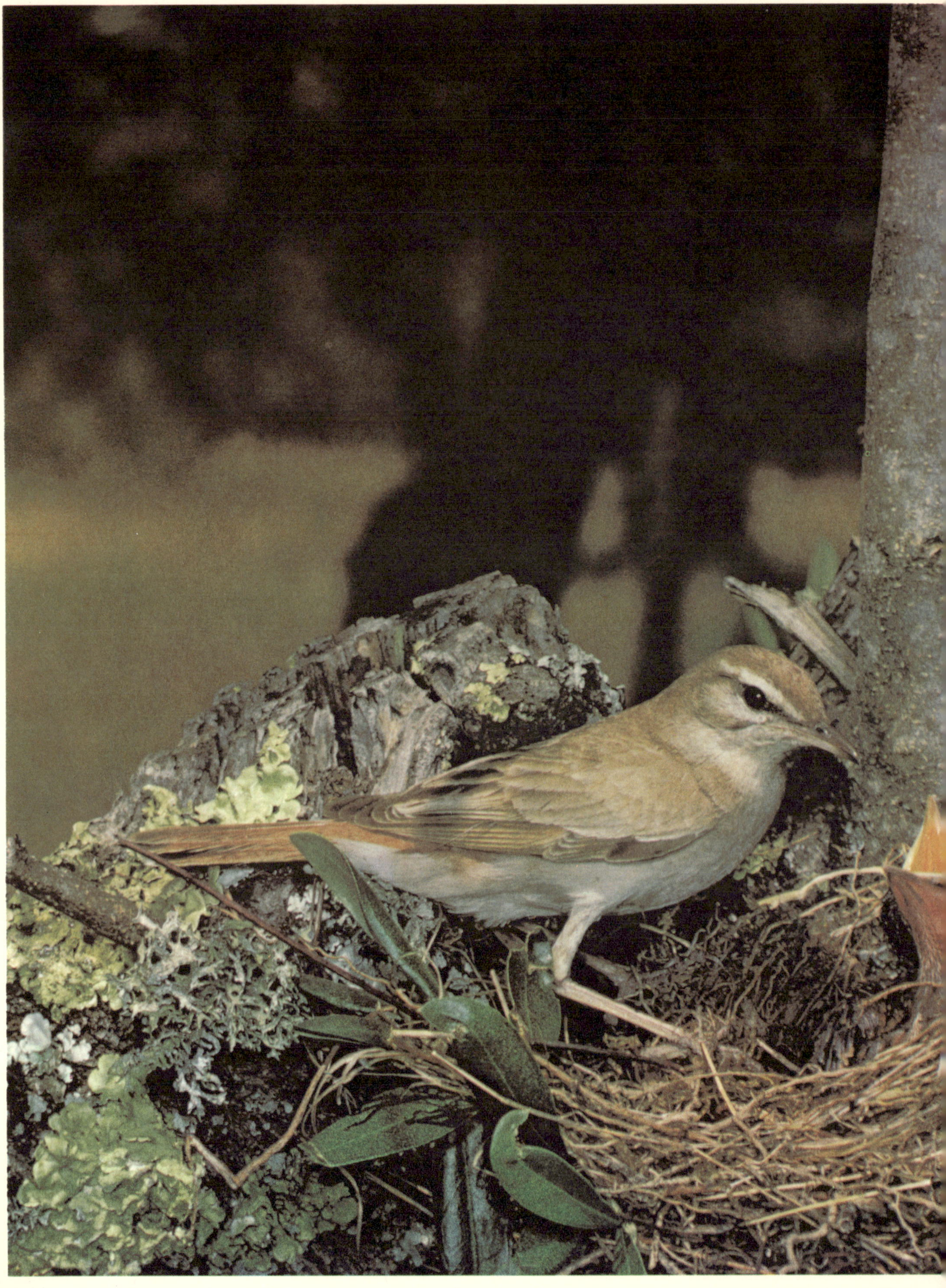

*Left* The **Rufous Bush Chat** (also called Bush-robin and Rufous Warbler) is here feeding its young in the nest which is often, like this one, so open and ill concealed that it seems surprising that any young escape the predators which abound in the places where it breeds. This species has a curious distribution, some being resident in the tropics, others breeding a long way further north but joining the tropical residents for the winter.

*Above* The **Common Fantail Warbler**, a 'little brown job', is another bird with a curious distribution. Mainly tropical or sub-tropical, from Africa across to south-eastern Asia, it also occurs along both north and south sides of the Mediterranean. There are over seventy species of fantail warbler, a high proportion of them in the tropics, and many so similar as to demand great expertise to distinguish them.

sheen, a bright yellow-ringed eye in a black head, a white band dividing a blue breast from a rusty-red belly and brilliant white below the wings and beside and below the upper part of the tail. No bird is more friendly-disposed towards man and its importuning attentions at out-of-doors meals would be a nuisance were it not so colourful and cheerful. Care should be taken not to confuse it with Hildebrant's Starling, which sometimes occurs in the same places and is very similar in plumage, though it lacks the white and has a more orange eye. Immature Superb Starlings are an even greater trap for the unwary, since they have no white breast-band and may easily be mistaken for Hildebrandt's, unless the white beneath the tail can be seen.

The sexes of most of the starling family are alike, but the Violet-backed, another very beautiful African species, and one of the smallest of the family, is a startling exception. The male has its entire upper-parts and breast a lovely deep metallic violet colour, while the female is a drab brown bird with spotted breast, and might well be taken for a different species altogether.

Birds which are usually grouped with the starlings are the two species of oxpecker or tick-bird, associated with the large mammals and domestic livestock of Africa. They spend much of their lives clinging to these creatures and climbing about them, searching for insect pests, investigating every nook and cranny and being especially attracted to sores and wounds, from which they apparently relish the blood and serous discharge. They travel in small flocks and fly from one group of animals to another with harsh cries; they seem to be well tolerated by their hosts, even such an irascible creature as the Black Rhinoceros taking little notice unless they venture into an eye or too far up a nostril. Elephants are an exception: curiously enough they will not stand the attentions of oxpeckers, but they ignore the Piapiac, a bird with somewhat similar habits, although it appears to use its host more as a perch than as an actual source of food, sallying off to catch small creatures distributed by its grazing vehicle.

Sunbirds and the closely related spider-hunters are small or very small birds with long thin de-curved bills. They are very active and in many ways show a resemblance to hummingbirds, although they are not closely related, especially since they feed on nectar and tiny insects, some being able to hover in front of a flower to feed, even though they more commonly perch to do so. The males of many species are beautifully coloured, with a metallic sheen on much of their plumage, but most females are dull brown or green, sometimes with streaks or spots.

There are over a hundred species of sunbirds and these are widespread over tropical Africa, and from India and Malaya to the Pacific islands and northern Australia. They build hanging, not very tidy, nests with an entrance near the top and often with a trailing 'tail' of fibres and leaves which makes an otherwise conspicuous nest appear like a collection of rubbish hanging from a tree. The nests of spider-hunters differ in being cup-shaped and protected by a broad leaf, to which the nest is sewn by fibres and cobwebs.

The tanagers are a large family of over 200 species, confined to the New World and especially to the tropical parts of it, although four species migrate far into North America to breed. They are mostly small birds, only a few species being as large as a thrush, and nearly all are gaily coloured. The principal food of the family is fruit and nectar, although many take insects as well. They therefore spend most of their life in the trees, inhabiting all types of growth from dense tall forest to low trees and scattered bushes, but apparently none regularly feed on the ground.

Most tanagers build open cup-shaped nests at varying heights, but a few species which are not entirely typical of the family use tree holes or build oval nests with an entrance in the side. The female alone incubates the eggs, usually closely attended by her mate which also helps in feeding the nestlings.

Although some people class them as a separate family, the beautiful little honey-creepers are really tanagers which have adapted themselves to live like sunbirds, their long slim bills enabling them to probe deep into flowers for the nectar and tiny insects to be found there. The male Red-legged Honey-creeper, a species which is found from Cuba and Mexico to Equador and Brazil, is a most gorgeous little blue bird with black wings and mantle, metallic greenish crown and red legs. The female is dull green and yellow. After the breeding season the male moults into the same drab plumage as his mate, which is an unusual occurrence in species of this family.

*Above* It is sometimes said that if a competition were to be held to determine the most beautiful bird in the tropics, the **Golden-breasted Starling** would easily win. There is no doubt that it is a most gorgeous bird but . . . if only it had not that glaring white eye!

*Left* The **Red-billed Oxpecker** is one of the two species of so-called 'tick-birds' which, closely related to the starlings, have adapted themselves to live clinging to large mammals as woodpeckers do to trees.

81

At the end of the list of the birds of the world come those which are usually lumped together as seed-eaters, the sparrows, finches, grosbeaks, cardinals, buntings waxbills and weavers. Many of these are found in the tropics: so many indeed that selection of a few for mention is very difficult.

Some of the most interesting – though by no means the most beautiful – members of this group are the fourteen species of Darwin's Finches, so called because they were discovered by Charles Darwin and greatly influenced him in his thinking about evolution. Found only on the Galapagos Islands (and one species on the Cocos Islands nearby), they illustrate probably better than any other group of birds how an animal will subdivide into a number of species, each adapted to fill a separate ecological niche. Not all Darwin's Finches are seed-eaters, some living on insects and others on nectar, and the beaks which they have developed to exploit these various sources of food constitute the chief way in which the various species of rather drab 'ordinary-looking' birds differ from each other. One of them has been given the name Woodpecker Finch because it clings to the vertical trunks of trees and is able to climb up them. Like a woodpecker, too, it digs into the wood for insects, but there the similarity ceases, since it has not the long beak nor the very long extensible tongue of a woodpecker. As a result it has developed a remarkable habit: having dug away the soft wood it picks up a cactus spine or thin sharp twig in its beak and pokes it into the cavity to dislodge the insect. As this emerges, it is seized by the bird, which drops the spike in order to do so.

Although Darwin's Finches have rather dull plumage, many seed-eaters are quite the opposite. The Gouldian Finch, from Northern Australia, must rank as one of the most beautiful of all birds. A green back, shading into a dark pointed tail at one end and into a blue band bordering a sharp line of demarcation from the scarlet face at the other, would be brilliant enough, but when the bird has a bright mauve breast and canary-yellow belly the effect is quite startling. However, as usual in nature, these apparently incompatible colours live quite harmoniously together. There are three natural forms of the Gouldian Finch, the Red, Black, and Yellow-headed, the last being seen much less frequently than the others. Closely related, though on the whole not so vividly coloured, are a handful of species of parrot-finches. They are bright green in body colour with red or blue in the head or tail, and are found in the Philippines, Papua and many Pacific Islands.

Africa and India have many species of the well-known weaver birds. They are noisy, sparrow-like, mainly highly gregarious birds and most of them build elaborate nests, woven with dried grasses and usually suspended from trees, bushes or reeds in vast communities. Some are in fact joined together as communal nests of great size like vast tenements, with entrances and passages leading to the nest chambers. The males of many of the African weavers have their main plumage colour bright yellow, with various patterns of black in the head and wings, by which the species may be differentiated. In most cases their mates are dowdy little greyish-brown birds like female House Sparrows.

One of the weavers, the Quelea, has so enormously increased in number that it has become a serious menace to African crops of small grain. These birds fly around in such immense numbers that they are sometimes mistaken for locusts; a million birds in one flock is nothing out of the ordinary. It has been estimated that a million birds can destroy sixty tons of growing wheat in a day. Many forms of control have been attempted, none very satisfactory as can be judged from the fact that in Tanzania *in one year* forty million nestlings were destroyed, with more than a further million adults at roosts, while in the same country *in the following year* thirty-two million nestlings and five and a half million adults were killed. In South Africa between January and March of that year seventy-five million youngsters were destroyed. But this almost unbelievable slaughter appeared to have little permanent effect on the numbers of the birds or on their appalling depredations.

# Photographing Birds

Visitors to the tropics will find it comparatively easy to photograph large birds such as storks and flamingos, but in most cases even experienced bird photographers have remarkable difficulty in bringing home satisfactory pictures of the smaller birds, except those few which will readily come down to a handful of crumbs or seeds. Occasionally the unexpected will happen and an otherwise difficult bird will offer an unusual opportunity. I had the good fortune to find, in Northern Territory Kenya, a male Red-billed Hornbill which was happy to feed its wife and youngsters, which were immured in a mudded-up hole in a tree, on sardine sandwiches which it snatched almost from my hand. Careful watching may show a favourite perch to which a kingfisher or bee-eater will repeatedly return (see pages 2 and 66) but a high proportion of species will remain unphotographed except by those few people who are able to stay in an area far longer than most visitors.

All the photographs which illustrate this book were taken with an ordinary 35mm reflex camera with 'through-the-lens' light meter and lenses of between 135mm and 400mm focal length. In fact good bird photographs can be taken with any miniature reflex camera to which a long-focus lens can be attached, and T-T-L metering is by no means essential, nor is it generally agreed that it is desirable. Although most of the photographs in this book were taken with the aid of one, it is particularly apposite in a book about the tropics that their complete infallibility should be questioned. This is not the place for a technical discussion on the optics or electronics of T-T-L meters, but it must be remembered that cameras differ in the means by which the light is 'fed' to the meter, and there is little doubt that in the tropics with the source of light almost directly overhead and with the light sometimes very bright indeed, some meters give much more accurate and reliable readings than others, even when allowance is made, as it must be, for the fact that the principal subject, the bird, is likely to occupy only a small proportion of the frame and will almost certainly have a different 'light value' from its surroundings or background. It need hardly be said that a bird silhouetted against the sky needs considerable compensation, plus both experience and luck, especially if it be a pure white bird such as the Little Egret on page 7.

I and some of my photographer friends have had bitter experience of meters, on quite expensive cameras and which had proved completely reliable in Europe and North America, becoming so erratic in tropical conditions as to waste an immense amount of film, to say nothing of the time and patience which had been expended. Perhaps even more galling was the fact that other friends in the party, using different but no more expensive cameras, had uniformly good results, apparently because their light meters were of a different design.

Thus one of the most important rules when photographing wildlife in the tropics is to know your light meter – it may be necessary (especially between ten o'clock in the morning and four in the afternoon) to make considerable allowance for overexposure. Preferably several shots should

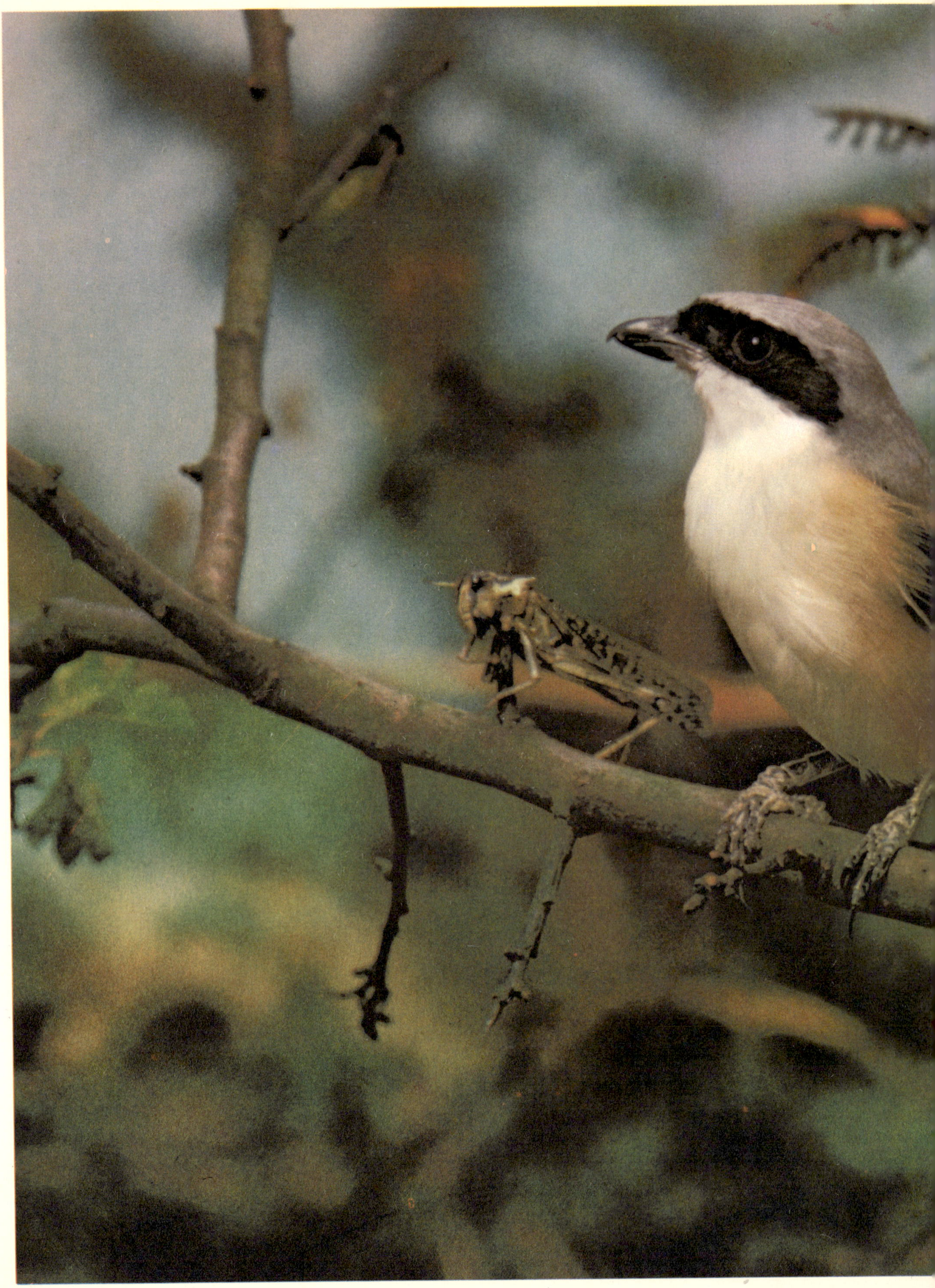

Many species of shrikes impale their prey on thorns or spikes – sometimes on barbed wire – either to make it easier to pull apart or to store it until it is needed. Here an Indian **Rufous-backed Shrike** has impaled a locust. The notes of shrikes are usually regarded as harsh and most unmusical, but some species – especially this one – are not only wonderful mimics but have a beautiful, quiet, rambling song, which cannot be better described than in the words of Salim Ali (see 'Books to read' on page 91) when he says it is 'uttered in the nature of a soliloquy'.

Shrikes are often very bold in defence of their nests and young, and the author was struck a number of sharp blows on the back of the head by the bird in the photograph.

be taken of each subject, using different exposures, but this is by no means always possible with a highly mobile subject.

Two principal methods are used to get close enough to such a wary and comparatively small quarry as a bird in order to obtain photographs: stalking with a long-focus lens, and using a hide in which the photographer can remain hidden while the bird approaches him, because the hide is placed overlooking something which particularly attracts it. Very commonly this is the bird's nest, though food is often used as bait. Sometimes the hide merely has a view over a likely piece of terrain, for example a pool or small island in an estuary.

The success of the hide placed near a nest is dependent, except in the case of a few very confiding species, upon the fact that birds cannot count. The photographer, having at least one assistant who will walk ostentatiously away from the hide when all is ready, leaves the birds ignorant of the fact that someone else has remained inside the hide. Although not so essential, this can also be an advantage at a 'wait and see' hide near food or other attraction, since birds do not always retire completely from the vicinity while the hide is being erected. In passing, it should be noted that it is a golden rule that the photographer must not emerge from a hide at a nest in the absence of a helper, because the shock of his sudden appearance may well cause the bird to desert its eggs or young. A similarly firm rule is that if a nervous bird has not returned to its nest within a given time, the hide should be vacated and, if necessary, dismantled or moved away. Preferably this should be done in the presence of the helper who can be 'called-up' by means of a pre-arranged signal, such as a handkerchief shown at the back of the hide. The time allowed for the bird's return will depend upon the photographer's experience and upon the species of the bird. For example, for a small bird such as a warbler or flycatcher, which feeds its young on insects carried in the bill, a period of more than half an hour would begin to be worrying, while with fairly well-grown young, an hour or longer is not at all abnormal with birds such as linnets or greenfinches, which feed by regurgitation. However, the age of the chicks, the weather and many other points must be taken into consideration.

Birds whose young are able to leave the nest shortly after hatching, such as waders, grebes, bustards and cranes, nearly always have to be photographed during incubation and, since the eggs of such species are usually placed on or near the ground in open situations, overheating by the sun is sometimes as great a hazard as chilling. It is often said that the 'dangerous period' is shortly before the eggs hatch. This is incorrect, especially in the case of larger birds. For example, there have been many records of the 'hard set' eggs of waders and similar species hatching successfully after being left for long periods, and even submerged by flood water for hours or even days; this might have proved fatal if it had occurred nearer the start of incubation. Thus, one of the most important attributes of the successful bird photographer is a sound knowledge of the way birds live.

It was formerly thought that a hide had to look like a natural object or be camouflaged if a close approach was to be made to a bird at its nest. Except for extremely wary species this is no longer believed by the majority of bird photographers: most now use some form of inconspicuously-coloured tent (usually rectangular) over a frame-work which can be dismantled. These may either be completely erected at a distance and moved closer as the bird becomes accustomed to them, or partially erected in the final position and their size gradually increased. Curiously enough, it is when photographing birds away from a nest, such as on a mudflat or other feeding place, that camouflage is of more advantage, since there is no real need for the bird to approach within range of the camera.

Until recently, it was an aphorism that a really stable tripod was an absolute essential in a bird photographer's outfit. Although this is still true of nest photography, the tripod is increasingly being abandoned for other types of work. For flight shots it is obviously impossible to use a tripod – for stalking almost so. However, a camera with a long and often heavy lens is not the easiest thing to hold steady, and various aids have been developed, such as the monopod, with its single leg either resting on the ground or, more usually, in a small pocket suspended over the chest by a strap around the neck, and the gun-stock for stabilizing against the shoulder. An aid to the ease of operation, though not altogether to stability, is pistol-grip focussing, while pistol-grip shutter-releases are frequently used.

In recent years a technique has become increasingly popular which is, in effect, a combination of hiding place and stalking.

This is the use of a motor car, and sometimes of a boat. If cautiously driven, a car does not immediately imply danger to a bird and sometimes an unexpectedly close approach may be made. It is, however, essential that no-one gets out; silence and slow movements within the car are also important.

A heavy lens is comparatively easy to use from a car with wind-up windows, the lens being rested on the top of the window, which of course is adjustable for height. Sliding windows are not so good, since the window-bottom is usually too low unless one kneels uncomfortably on the floor of the car. Very helpful is a bracket which grips the window-bottom and has a U-shaped rest for the lens. Those cars with fixed windows except for the driver and front passenger are a nuisance and to be avoided if more than two photographers are involved, although it is surprising how little effect even a dirty window has if the lens is pressed tight up against it. The photograph of the sandgrouse on page 43 was taken through a windscreen which was anything but clean. However, this is no help so far as support and stability are concerned and a winding window is by far the best. Some people use a piece of sponge rubber between the top of the glass and the lens, partly to protect both of these and partly to dampen vibration. It is my experience that sponge rubber, by its very resilience, is inclined to *increase* camera-shake rather than reduce it. Whatever type of support is used, there is no doubt that a short exposure is the best aid in defeating camera-shake.

This raises the question of the type of film to be used. Short exposures mean fast films and – so far as colour films are concerned – the faster the film the less consistent the results are likely to be. After many years of very mixed experience with different types of colour film I am coming more and more to the conclusion that, for the kind of photography being discussed, fast colour film should be used only when a slow one is quite useless; when the light gives no meter reading at all (for the lens to be used) at, say 1/30 second, or when movement of the subject absolutely demands a shutter speed for which the slow film is totally inadequate. Even then, I am very inclined to take no photograph at all if my slow film will not do. Since Kodachrome II must be known the world over, there seems to be no harm in saying that I take with me 'on safari' a hundred cassettes of Kodachrome II to every ten of high speed film and the latter as often as not come home un-exposed, not because the sun always shone, but ten shots at 1/30 second – even hand-held – on the former are more likely to give one really acceptable result than ten at 1/250 second on the latter. On the other hand there are exceptions: the plate on page 46 would not be there had it not been for High Speed Ektachrome.

Mention must be made of electronic flash. So far as birds are concerned, its principal uses are for photography at the nest and the 'studio' type of shot mentioned later, although it is by no means to be scorned when birds can be attracted to food or a drinking or bathing pool. It can be used either as a 'boost' for indifferent daylight or as the main light source. Each has its snags: the former is prone to give a 'double image' of a fidgety bird, and the latter all-too-easily makes a photograph appear as though it had been taken in the middle of the night.

Three other methods of obtaining bird photographs must not be forgotten. The first method involves use of the photo-electric cell which operates the shutter of the camera and/or fires a flash as the bird approaches a given point. The second utilizes the long pneumatic or electric shutter-release which may be operated by the photographer from a distance. Using it in conjunction with an electric film-wind is essential, although few makes of camera have these and they are very expensive, but, without one, the need for the operator to visit the camera after each exposure is a quite indefensible disturbance to the birds. The third method is 'studio' photography, which is the taking of photographs in captivity or in 'controlled' conditions. Compared with the immense pleasure to be obtained from photographing any form of creature 'free and wild', photography in zoos and private collections is an unexciting business but there are occasions when, for illustrative purposes, it becomes almost essential. For example, although hummingbirds can be photographed in the wild, it is remarkably difficult to do so and most of the best photographs of members of this family have been taken in controlled conditions. Many birds, although not uncommon in captivity, live in places which are difficult of access or most unsuitable for photography and illustrations of them would be few and far between were

**Red-legged** or **Blue Honey-creeper** and **Yellow-winged Sugarbird** are alternative names for the lovely little bird illustrated above. A male is shown here in his gaudiest plumage, since out of the breeding season he will moult into the dull green in which the female is clad all the year round. Most honey-creepers are not renowned for their songs, which in many cases are little more than rather faint squeaks. They feed by sucking nectar from flowers and on small insects, and to some extent on soft fruit.

**Reichenow's Weaver.** There are many species of weaver in Asia and Africa and not a few, especially the males, have brilliant yellow in their plumage. Their names are not always much more helpful in recognition than is the name of their discoverer — for example, the African Black-headed, Masked, Spectacled and Black-necked Weavers are all yellow birds with black on the head, and so are Reichenow's, Speke's and Layard's — and a 'field guide' is the only hope of recognition except to the very experienced bird-watcher.

advantage not taken of the fact that many of them are comparatively well-known as cage or aviary birds.

One of the great disadvantages inherent in a high proportion of 'studio' pictures is that they almost inevitably include wire-netting, brick walls or artificial-looking perches. Such pictures are better than nothing, but most of them can hardly be described as satisfactory. On the other hand, obvious wire-netting is better than a 'mock-up' which is intended to mislead the viewer into thinking that a caged bird was photographed in the wild, and it is my most firm belief that such photographs should frankly be declared as such to avoid any possibility of misunderstanding.

However, this is not to say – bearing that proviso in mind – that it is not desirable to make a photograph of a captive bird *appear* as though it had been taken in natural surroundings, even if for purely aesthetic reasons. It has long been the practice to photograph reptiles in the confines of what can best be described as a studio – often little more than a low wall temporarily erected around a small area of their habitat – and few would question that such pictures are infinitely preferable to those showing a concrete or tiled enclosure. The ability of the majority of birds to fly makes such a method impracticable in their case, but an extension of this principle which adds a confining roof and, usually, a natural background of plants or even coloured photographs of foliage, may be the only reasonable means of obtaining an illustration of an otherwise nearly impossible subject. It should be added that in no circumstances should wild birds be subjected to this method during the breeding season.

In an age when man is rapidly destroying not only his own habitat but also inevitably that of the wildlife around him, bird photographers have a great responsibility, whatever method they employ, not to endanger even further the already hazardous lives of the creatures of which they are trying to secure pictures. The welfare of the subject must always be the first consideration of the photographer – the attitude of a 'photo at any price' must never come into the photographing of wildlife.

# Books to Read

A detailed bibliography does not seem appropriate in a book such as this, especially since it would include papers and books not readily available to the general public. The list which follows is of books to which the author is especially indebted or which he feels will be useful to those poeple whose interest has been stimulated by this necessarily very superficial glance at the birds of the tropics. Some are unfortunately out of print, but most may be borrowed from a good library. They are divided according to the regions on the map on page 5. If there be any one book which deals, even in a condensed form, not only with tropical but all other birds, their anatomy and physiology, the way they live and are distributed over the world, and their scientific classification, it is *A New Dictionary of Birds*, edited by Sir Landsborough Thomson, and this cannot be too strongly recommended both as a reference book and as providing absorbing reading.

Although the last two books in the list are not entirely about birds, they are included because they contain guides to the National Parks and Nature Reserves of the world.

*Birds of Borneo* by B. E. Smythies. Oliver & Boyd, Edinburgh, 1968.

*Birds of East and Central Africa* by J. G. Williams. Collins, London.

*Birds of Surinam* by F. Haverschmidt. Oliver & Boyd, Edinburgh, 1968.

*Birds of Trinidad and Tobago* by G. A. C. Herklots. Collins, London, 1961.

*Birds of West and Equatorial Africa* by D. A. Bannerman. Oliver & Boyd, Edinburgh, 1953.

*Birds of the West Indies* by J. Bond. Collins, London, 1960.

*Book of Indian Birds* by Salim Ali. Bombay N.H.S.

*Darwin's Finches* by D. Lack. Cambridge University Press.

*Field Guide to Australian Birds* (2 vols) by P. Slater. Oliver & Boyd, Edinburgh, 1971.

*Guide to the Birds of Ceylon* by G. M. Henry. Oxford University Press, 1955.

*Guide to the Birds of South America* by R. M. De Schauensee. Oliver & Boyd, Edinburgh, 1971.

*Handbook of New Guinea Birds* by E. T. Gilliard and A. L. Rand. Weidenfeld and Nicholson, London, 1967.

*Popular Handbook of Indian Birds* by H. Whistler. Oliver & Boyd, Edinburgh, 1963.

*What Bird is That?* (Australia) by N. W. Cayley. Angus & Robertson, London, 1966.

**General**

*Birds of Prey* by G. and D. Lloyd. Hamlyn, London, 1969.

*Birds of the World* by Oliver L. Austin. Hamlyn, London, 1968.

*Coloured Key to the Wildfowl of the World* by Sir P. Scott. Witherby, London, 1969.

*New Dictionary of Birds* edited by Sir A. Landsborough Thomson. Nelson, London, 1964.

*Pigeons and Doves of the World* by D. Goodwin. British Museum (Natural History), London, 1967.

*Tropical Birds* by C. Roots. Hamlyn, London, 1971.

*Man and Wildlife* by C. A. W. Guggisberg. Evans, London, 1970.

*World Wildlife Guide*. Threshold Books, London, 1971.

**White-browed Sparrow-weaver** is an unwieldy name for a small bird, but an apt one. This species is locally very common and some trees are absolutely festooned with their nests. Although not brightly clad, it has a cheerful charm and sings a surprisingly tuneful, chortling song which might easily be mistaken for that of a starling. In some places they have taken to living near houses and compete with the other birds which feed on kitchen scraps.

# *Index*

The letters A, B, C and D refer to the tropical zones shown in the map on page 5. Page numbers in italic refer to illustrations. Spp. means 'various species' and is used where no particular species is mentioned in the text.

Adjutant Stork *Leptoptilos dubius* C 26
African Fish Eagle *Cuncuma vocifer* B 36
African Grey Parrot *Psittacus erithacus* B 54
African Jacana *Actophilornis africanus* B *35*, 48
American Black Vulture *Coragyps atratus* A 31
Anhinga *Anhinga rufa* ABC 7, 22
Augur Buzzard *Buteo rufofuscus* B *25*, 37
Australian Pelican *Pelecanus conspicillatus* D 19
Azure Nuthatch *Sitta azurea* C 73

Banded Pitta *Pitta guajana* C *71*
Barbet, D'Arnaud's *Trachyphonus darnaudii* B 69
Barbet, Gaudy *Megalaima mystacophanes* C 69
Barn Owl *Tyto alba* ABCD 40
Bay-backed Shrike *Lanius vittatus* C 77
Beautiful Nuthatch *Sitta formosa* C 73
Bee-eater, White-throated *Aerops albicollis* B 63, 65, *66*
Belted Kingfisher *Ceryle alcyon* A 62
Black-faced Sandgrouse *Eremialector decoratus* B *43*
Black Heron *Hydranassa ardesiaca* B 23
Black Kite *Milvus migrans* BCD 33
Black-necked Grebe *Podiceps nigricollis* B 18
Black-shouldered Kite (Black-winged Kite) *Elanus caeruleus* ABCD *21*, 33
Blacksmith Plover *Hoplopterus armatus* B *38*, 50
Black Stork *Ciconia nigra* B 23
Black Swan *Chenopsis atrata* D 27
Black-winged Kite *Elanus caeruleus* ABCD *21*, 33
Black-winged Stilt *Himantopus himantopus* ABCD 50
Broadbill spp. BC 72
Broad-billed Roller *Eurystomus glaucurus* B 65
Brown Pelican *Pelecanus occidentalis* A 19
Budgerigar *Melopsittacus undulatus* D 54
Buff-backed Heron *Bubulcus ibis* ABCD 23
Bush Chat, Rufous *Cercotrichas galactotes* B 76, *78*
Bustard, Kori *Ardeotis kori* B *32*, 45
Buzzard, Augur *Buteo rufofuscus* B *25*, 37

Cassowary *Casuarius casuarius* D 13
Cattle Egret *Bubulcus ibis* ABCD 23
Chestnut-bellied Nuthatch *Sitta caslania* C 76

Cockatoo, Leadbeater's *Cacatua leadbeateri* D 51
Cockatoo, Palm (Great Black) *Probosciger aterrimus* D 51
Cock-of-the-Rock *Rupicola peruviana* A 72
Common Cormorant *Phalacrocorax carbo* ABCD 22
Common Crane *Grus grus* BC 41
Common Swift *Apus apus* B(winter) 58
Condor *Vultur gryphus* A 31
Cormorant, Common *Phalacrocorax carbo* ABCD 22
Cotinga spp. A 72
Coucal *Centropus sinensis* C 52, 54
Crane, Common *Grus grus* 41
**Crane, Crowned** *Balearica regulorum* B *29*, 41, 44
Crane, Sarus *Grus antigone* C 44
Crane, Siberian White *Grus leucogeranus* 44
Crimson Rosella *Platycercus elegans* D *47*, 54
Crowned Crane *Balearica regulorum* B *29*, 41, 44
Crowned Plover *Stephanibyx coronatus* B 50
Crow-pheasant *Centropus sinensis* C *52*, 54
Crow spp. BCD 73

D'Arnaud's Barbet *Trachyphonus darnaudii* B 69
Darter *Anhinga rufa* ABC 7, 22
Darwin's Finch spp. A 82
Doherty's Bush Shrike *Telephorus dohertyi* B 77
Dollar Bird *Eurystomus orientalis* CD 65
Dove, Spotted *Streptopelia chinensis* C *43*
Duck, White-faced Tree *Dendrocygna viduata* AB *20*, 37

Eagle, African Fish *Cuncuma vocifer* B 36
Eagle, Long-crested (Hawk) *Lophoaetus occipitalis* B *25*, 37
Edible-nest Swiftlet spp. CD 59
Egret, Cattle *Bubulcus ibis* ABCD 23
Egret, Great or Large *Egretta alba* ABCD 23
Egret, Little *Egretta garzetta* BCD 7, 23
Egret, Reddish *Hydranassa rufescens* A 23
Egret, Yellow-billed *Mesophoyx intermedius* BC 23
Egyptian Goose *Alopochen aegyptiacus* B 27
Egyptian Vulture *Neophron percnopterus* BC 36
Emu *Dromaius novaehollandiae* D 13
European Roller *Coracias garrulus* B(winter) *60–1*, 65
Everglade Kite *Rostrhamus sociabilis* A *8*, 33

Fairy Tern *Gygis alba* BCD 50
Falcon, Laughing *Herpetotheres cachinnans* A 37
Falcon, Peregrine *Falco peregrinus* BCD 31

93

Fantail Warbler *Cisticola juncidis* BCD 76, *79*
Finch, Darwin's spp. A 82
Finch, Gouldian *Poephila gouldiae* D 82
Finch, Parrot spp. D 82
Finch, Woodpecker *Camarhynchus pallidus* A 82
Flamingo, Greater *Phoenicopterus ruber* ABC *17*, 27
Flamingo, Lesser *Phoeniconaias minor* BC *14*, 27
Flamingo spp. 26
Four-coloured Bush Shrike *Telephorus quadricolor* B 77
Frigate Bird spp. ABCD 22

Galapagos Hawk *Buteo galapagoensis* A 37
Gallinule, Purple *Porphyrio porphyrio* BCD *34*, 45
Garganey *Anas guerquedula* BC(winter) 30
Gaudy Barbet *Megalaima mystacophanes* C 69
Giant Hummingbird *Patagona gigas* A 59
Glossy Ibis *Plegadis falcinellus* ABCD *14*, 26
Golden-breasted Starling *Cosmopsarus regius* B 77, *81*
Goose, Egyptian *Alopochen aegyptiacus* B 27
Goose, Hawaiian (Néné) *Branta sandvicensis* A 27
Gouldian Finch *Poephila gouldiae* D 82
Great Black Cockatoo *Probosciger aterrimus* D 51
Great Crested Grebe *Podiceps cristatus* BD 18
Great Egret *Egretta alba* ABCD 23
Greater Flamingo *Phoenicopterus ruber* ABC *17*, 27
Grebe, Black-necked *Podiceps nigricollis* B 18
Grebe, Great Crested *Podiceps cristatus* BD 18
Grebe, Little *Podiceps ruficollis* BCD 18
Grebe, Pied-billed *Podilymbus podiceps* A 19
Green Heron *Butorides virescens* A 22
Green Magpie *Cissa chinensis* C 73
Grey-headed Gull *Larus cirrocephalus* B 50
Grey Heron *Ardea cinerea* BCD 22
Ground Cuckoo, Renauld's *Cartococcyx renauldi* C *49*
Ground Hornbill *Bucorvus leadbeateri* B 69
Ground Parrot *Pezoporus wallicus* D 51
Gull, Grey-headed *Larus cirrocephalus* B 50
Hammerhead *Scopus umbretta* B 23
Hammerhead Stork *Scopus umbretta* B 23
Hawaiian Goose *Branta sandvicensis* A 27
Hawk, Galapagos *Buteo galapagoensis* A 37
Helmeted Hornbill *Rhinoplax vigil* C 68
Heron, Black *Hydranassa ardesiaca* B 23
Heron, Buff-backed *Bubulcus ibis* ABCD 23

Heron, Green *Butorides virescens* A 22
Heron, Grey *Ardea cinerea* BCD 22
Heron, Night *Nycticorax nycticorax* ABCD 23
Hildebrandt's Starling *Spreo hildebrandti* B 80
Hill Mynah *Gracula religiosa* C 77
Honey-creeper, Red-legged *Cyanerpes cyaneus* A 80, *88*
Hooded Vulture *Necrosyrtes monachus* B 36
Hoopoe *Upupa epops* BC 65
Hornbill, Ground *Bucorvus leadbeateri* B 69
Hornbill, Helmeted *Rhinoplax vigil* C 68
Hornbill, Red-billed *Tockus erythrorhynchus* B *67*, 69
Hottentot Teal *Anas punctata* B 30
Hummingbird, Giant *Patagona gigas* A 59
Hummingbird, Rubythroat *Archilochus colubris* A 59
Hummingbird, Streamertail *Trochilus polytmus* A *53*

Ibis, Glossy *Plegadis falcinellus* ABCD *14*, 26
Ibis, Sacred *Threskiornis aethiopicus* B *15*, 26, 27
Ibis, Scarlet *Eudocimus ruber* A 26
Ibis, Wood (Yellow-billed Stork) *Ibis ibis* B *11*, 26
Inca Tern *Larosterna inca* A 50
Indian Roller *Coracias benghalensis* C 65
Indian Tree Pie *Dendrocitta vagabunda* C *64*

Jacana, African *Actophilornis africanus* B *35*, 48
Jacana, Pheasant-tailed *Hydrophasianus chirurgus* C 48

Kentish Plover *Charadrius alexandrinus* ABCD 48
King Bird of Paradise *Ciccinurus regius* D 73
Kingfisher, Belted *Ceryle alcyon* A 62
Kingfisher, Malachite *Corythornis cristata* B *2-3*, 62
Kingfisher, Pied *Ceryle rudis* BC 62
Kingfisher, White-breasted *Halcyon smyrnensis* C *56*, 62
King Vulture (American) *Sarcorhamphus papa* A 31
King Vulture (Asian) *Torgos calvus* C 31
Kite, Black *Milvus migrans* BCD 33
Kite, Black-shouldered (Black-winged) *Elanus caeruleus* ABCD *21*, 33
Kite, Everglade *Rostrhamus sociabilis* A *8*, 33
Kittlitz's Sand Plover *Charadrius pecuarius* B 50
Kookaburra *Dacelo novaeguineae* D 62
Kori Bustard *Ardeotis kori* B *32*, 45

Lappet-faced Vulture *Torgos tracheliotus* B 36
Lapwing, Red-wattled *Vanellus indicus* C *39*, 50
Large Egret *Egretta alba* ABCD 23

Laughing Falcon *Herpetotheres cachinnans* A 37
Leadbeater's Cockatoo *Cacatua leadbeateri* D 51
Lesser Flamingo *Phoeniconaias minor* BC 14, 27
Lilac-breasted Roller *Coracias caudata* B 65, *66*
Lily-trotter (African) *Actophilornis africanus* B *35*, 48
Little Egret *Egretta garzetta* BCD 7, 23
Little Grebe *Podiceps ruficollis* BCD 18
Little Ringed Plover *Charadrius dubius* CD 48
Long-crested Eagle *Lophoaetus occipitalis* B *25*, 37
Long-tailed Manakin *Chiroxiphia linearis* A *70*
Lorikeet, Rainbow *Trichoglossus haematodus* D 51

Magpie, Green *Cissa chinensis* C 73
Malachite Kingfisher *Corythornis cristata* B *2–3*, 62
Manakin, Long-tailed *Chiroxiphia linearis* A *70*
Manakin spp. A 72
Mannikin spp. BCD 72
Marabou Stork *Leptoptilos crumeniferus* B 23, 26, 36
Motmot, Swainson's *Momotus momota bahamensis* A 57
Mute Swan *Cygnus olor* 27
Mynah, Hill *Gracula religiosa* C 77

Néné (Hawaiian Goose) *Branta sandvicensis* A 27
Night Heron *Nycticorax nycticorax* ABCD 23
Nuthatch, Azure *Sitta azurea* C 73
Nuthatch, Beautiful *Sitta formosa* C 73
Nuthatch, Chestnut-bellied *Sitta castania* C 76
Nuthatch, Velvet-fronted *Sitta frontalis* C 73

Osprey *Pandion haliaetus* ABCD 31
Ostrich *Struthio camelus* B 13
Owl, Barn *Tyto alba* ABCD 40
Owl, Verreaux's Eagle *Bubo lacteus* B 40
Owl, White-faced Scops *Otus leucotis* B 40
Oxpecker, Red-billed *Buphagus erythrorhynchus* B 80, *81*

Painted Stork *Ibis leucocephalus* C *11*, 26
Palm Cockatoo *Probosciger aterrimus* D 51
Palm Swift *Cypsiurus parvus* BC 59
Paradise, King Bird of *Ciccinurus regius* D 73
Parrakeet, Pennant's *Platycercus elegans* D *47*, 54
Parrakeet, Ring-necked *Psittacula krameri* BC *46*, 54
Parrot, African Grey *Psittacus erithacus* B 54
Parrot Finch spp. D 82
Parrot, Ground *Pezoporus wallicus* D 51
Pelican, Australian *Pelecanus conspicillatus* D 19

Pelican, Brown *Pelecanus occidentalis* A 19
Pelican, Pink-backed *Pelecanus rufescens* B 19
Pelican, White *Pelecanus onocrotalus* B *6*, 19
Pennant's Parrakeet *Platycercus elegans* BC *46*, 54
Peregrine Falcon *Falco peregrinus* BCD 31
Pheasant-tailed Jacana *Hydrophasianus chirurgus* C 48
Pied-billed Grebe *Podilymbus podiceps* A 19
Pied Kingfisher *Ceryle rudis* BC 62
Pie, Indian Tree *Dendrocitta vagabunda* C *64*
Pink-backed Pelican *Pelecanus rufescens* B 19
Pitta, Banded *Pitta guajana* C *71*
Pitta spp. BCD 73
Plover, Blacksmith *Hoplopterus armatus* B *38*, 50
Plover, Crowned *Stephanibyx coronatus* B 50
Plover, Kentish *Charadrius alexandrinus* ABCD 48
Plover, Kittlitz's Sand *Charadrius pecuarius* B 50
Plover, Little Ringed *Charadrius dubius* CD 48
Pondicherry Vulture *Torgos calvus* C 31
Purple Gallinule *Porphyrio porphyrio* BCD *34*, 45

Quelea *Quelea quelea* B 82

Rainbow Lorikeet *Trichoglossus haematodus* D 51
Red-billed Hornbill *Tockus erythrorhynchus* B *67*, 69
Red-billed Oxpecker *Buphagus erythrorhynchus* B 80, *81*
Reddish Egret *Hydranessa rufescens* A 23
Red-legged Honey-creeper *Cyanerpes cyaneus* A 80, *88*
Red-wattled Lapwing *Vanellus indicus* C *39*, 50
Reichenow's Weaver *Othyphantes reichenowi* B 89
Renauld's Ground Cuckoo *Cartococcyx renauldi* C 49
Rhea *Rhea americana* A 13
Ring-necked Parrakeet *Psittacula krameri* BC *46*, 54
Robin Chat, Ruppell's *Cossypha semirufa* B *74–5*, 76
Robin Chat, White-browed *Cossypha heuglini* B 76
Roller, Broad-billed *Eurystomus glaucurus* B 65
Roller, European *Coracias garrulus* B(winter) *60–1*, 65
Roller, Indian *Coracias benghalensis* C 65
Roller, Lilac-breasted *Coracias caudata* B 65, *66*
Rosella, Crimson *Platycercus elegans* D *47*, 54
Ruby-throat Hummingbird *Archilochus colubris* A 59

Rufous-backed Shrike *Lanius schach* C 77, *84–5*
Rufous Bush Chat *Cercotrichas galactotes* B 76, *78*
Ruppell's Robin Chat *Cossypha semirufa* B *74–5*, 76

Sacred Ibis *Threskiornis aethiopicus* B *15*, 26, 27
Saddlebill Stork *Ephippiorhynchus senegalensis* B *10*, 26
Sandgrouse, Black-faced *Eremialector decoratus* B *43*
Sandpiper, Wood *Tringa glareola* BCD(winter) *32*, 50
Sarus Crane *Grus antigone* C 44
Scarlet Ibis *Eudocimus ruber* A 26
Secretary Bird *Sagittarius serpentarius* B *28*, 37
Shoebill Stork *Balaeniceps rex* B 23
Shoveler *Anas clypeata* BC(winter) 30
Shrike, Bay-backed *Lanius vittatus* C 77
Shrike, Doherty's Bush *Telephorus dohertyi* B 77
Shrike, Four-coloured Bush *Telephorus quadricolor* B 77
Shrike, Rufous-backed *Lanius schach* C 77, *84–5*
Siberian White Crane *Grus leucogeranus* C 44
Snake Bird (Darter) *Anhinga rufa* ABC 7, 22
Spiderhunter spp. C 80
Spotted Dove *Streptopelia chinensis* C *43*
Starling, Golden-breasted *Cosmopsarus regius* B 77, *81*
Starling, Hildebrandt's *Spreo hildebrandti* B 80
Starling, Superb *Spreo superbus* B 77
Starling, Violet-backed *Cinnyricinclus leucogaster* B 80
Stilt, Black-winged *Himantopus himantopus* ABCD 50
Stork, Adjutant *Leptoptilos dubius* C 26
Stork, Black *Ciconia nigra* B 23
Stork, Hammerhead *Scopus umbretta* B 23
Stork, Marabou *Leptoptilos crumeniferus* B 23, 26, 36
Stork, Painted *Ibis leucocephalus* C *11*, 26
Stork, Saddlebill *Ephippiorhynchus senegalensis* B *10*, 26
Stork, Shoebill *Balaeniceps rex* B 23
Stork, Whale-headed *Balaeniceps rex* B 23
Stork, White *Ciconia ciconia* BC(C winter) 23
Stork, Yellow-billed (Wood Ibis) *Ibis ibis* B *11*, 26
Streamertail Hummingbird *Trochilus polytmus* A *53*
Sunbird spp. BCD 80
Sunbittern *Eurypyga helias* A *32*
Superb Starling *Spreo superbus* B 77
Swainson's Motmot *Momotus momota bahamensis* A *57*
Swan, Black *Coscoroba atratus* D 27
Swan, Mute *Cygnus olor* 27
Swift, Common *Apus apus* B(winter) 58

Swift, Palm *Cypsiurus parvus* BC 59
Swiftlet, Edible-nest spp. CD 59

Tanager spp. A 80
Teal, Hottentot *Anas punctata* B 30
Tern, Fairy *Gygis alba* BCD 50
**Tern, Inca** *Larosterna inca* **A 50**
Toucan spp. A 69
Tree Pie, Indian *Dendrocitta vagabunda* C *64*

Velvet-fronted Nuthatch *Sitta frontalis* C 73
Verreaux's Eagle Owl *Bubo lacteus* B 40
Violet-backed Starling *Cinnyricinclus leucogaster* B 80
Vulture, American Black *Coragyps atratus* A 31
Vulture, Egyptian *Neophron percnopterus* BC 36
Vulture, Hooded *Necrosyrtes monachus* B 36
Vulture, King (American) *Sarcorhamphus papa* A 31
Vulture, King (Asian) *Torgos calvus* C 31
Vulture, Lappet-faced *Torgos tracheliotus* B 36
Vulture, Pondicherry *Torgos calvus* C 31
Vulture, White-backed *Pseudogyps africanus* B 36
Vulture, White-backed *Pseudogyps bengalensis* C *24*

Warbler, Fantail *Cisticola juncides* BCD 76, *79*
Weaver, Reichenow's *Othyphantes reichenowi* B *89*
Weaver, White-browed Sparrow *Plocepasser mahali* B *92*
**Weaver spp. BC 82**
Whale-headed Stork *Balaeniceps rex* B 23
White-backed Vulture *Pseudogyps africanus* B 36
White-backed Vulture *Pseudogyps bengalensis* C *24*
White-breasted Kingfisher *Halcyon smyrnensis* C 56, *62*
White-browed Robin Chat *Cossypha heuglini* B 76
White-browed Sparrow Weaver *Plocepasser mahali* B *92*
White-faced Scops Owl *Otus leucotis* B 40
White-faced Tree Duck *Dendrocygna viduata* AB *20*, 37
White Pelican *Pelecanus onocrotalus* B 6, *19*
White Stork *Ciconia ciconia* BC(C winter) 23
White-throated Bee-eater *Aerops albicollis* B 63, 65, *66*
Wood Ibis *Ibis ibis* B *11*, 26
Woodpecker Finch *Camarhynchus pallidus* A 82
Wood Sandpiper *Tringa glareola* BCD (winter) *32*, 50

Yellow-billed Egret *Mesophoyx intermedius* BC 23
Yellow-billed Stork *Ibis ibis* B *11*, 26